DATE DUE		
JA 17 '02			
MR 22 '05			
DE 17 '07			
APR 2 2 '08			
NOV 1 1 '70			

Using and Understanding Maps

Languages
of the World

Consulting Editor
Scott E. Morris
College of Mines and Earth Resources
University of Idaho

Chelsea House Publishers
New York   Philadelphia

This Publication was designed, edited and computer generated by
Lovell Johns Limited
10 Hanborough Business Park
Long Hanborough
Witney
Oxon, England OX8 8LH

The contents of this volume are based on the latest data available at the
time of publication.

Map credit: *Antarctica source map prepared at 1:20,000 by the British
Antarctic Survey Mapping and Geographic Information Centre, 1990.*

Cover credit: *Harold and Erica Van Pelt, Photographers, Los Angeles*

Printed in Mexico

 3 5 7 9 8 6 4 2

Library of Congress Cataloging in Publication Data

Languages of the world/editorial consultant, Scott Morris:
         p. cm. (Using and understanding maps)
         Includes glossary and index/gazetteer.
         Includes bibliographical references.
         Summary: Eighteen map spreads show the distribution and use
         of the major languages of the world.
         ISBN 0-7910-1811-3.   ISBN 0-7910-1824-5 (pbk.)
1. Linguistic geography — Maps. 2. Language and languages — Maps.
[1. Language and languages — Maps. 2. Atlases.]
         I. Morris. Scott Edward. II. Chelsea House Publishers. III. Series.
         G1046.E3L3 1993 <G&M>
         409 — dc20   92-22287
                                                        CIP
                                                        MAP AC

Introduction

We inhabit a fascinating and mysterious planet where the earth's physical features, life-forms, and the diversity of human culture conspire to produce a breathtaking environment. We don't have to travel very far to see and experience the wealth of this diverse planet; in fact, we don't have to travel at all. Everywhere images of the world are abundantly available in books, newspapers, magazines, movies, television, and the arts. We could say that *everywhere* one looks, our world is a brilliant moving tapestry of shapes, colors, and textures, and our experience of its many messages — whether in our travels or simply by gazing out into our own backyards — is what we call reality.

Geography is the study of a portion of that reality. More so, it is the study of how the physical and biological components (rocks, animals, plants, and people) of our planet are distributed and how they are interconnected. Geographers seek to describe and to explain the physical patterns that have evolved on the earth and also to discover the significance in the ways they have evolved. To do this, geographers rely on maps.

Maps can be powerful images. They convey selective information about vast areas of an overwhelmingly cluttered world. The cartographer, or mapmaker, must carefully choose the theme of a map, that is, what it will show, knowing that a good map will convey the essence of information while at the same time making the information easy to comprehend.

This volume and its companions in UNDERSTANDING AND USING MAPS are about the planet we call earth and the maps we use to find our way along its peaks and valleys. Each volume displays map images that reveal how the world is arranged according to a specific theme such as population, industries or the endangered world. The maps in each volume are accompanied by an interesting collection of facts — some are rather obvious, others are oddities. Yet all are meant to be informative.

Along with a wealth of facts, there are explanations of the various attributes and phenomena depicted by the maps. This information is provided to better understand the significance of the maps as well as to demonstrate how the many themes relate.

Names for places are essential to geographers. To study the world without devising names for places would be extremely difficult. But geographers also know that names are in no way permanent; place names change as people change. The recent reunification of Germany and the breakup of what was the Soviet Union — events that seem colossal from the perspective of socioeconomics — to geographers are simply events that require the drawing or erasing of one or a few boundaries and the renaming of one or several land masses. The geographer is constantly reminded that the world is in flux; a map is always in danger of being rendered obsolete by a turn in current events.

Because the world is dynamic, it continues to captivate the mind and stimulate the imagination. USING AND UNDERSTANDING MAPS presents the world as it is today, with the reservation that any dramatic rearrangement of land and people is likely, indeed inevitable, thus requiring the making of a new map. In this way maps are themselves a part of the evolutionary process.

Scott E. Morris

Languages of the World

Language has been defined as "a systematic means of communicating ideas or feelings by the use of conventionalized signs, gestures, marks or vocal sounds." Whatever the formal definition, it is clear that language is a fundamental aspect of culture — and culture is what distingishes the multitude of peoples on earth. Language is very important to the maintenance of a culture because it is the primary means of passing on, and thus preserving, a way of life for generations.

The geography of language, and of the variations of languages called dialects, tells us much more about the evolution of cultures. The mere fact that there are more than 3,000 languages in use today is testimony to the complex mosaic of peoples and cultures in our world. Given the enormous number of languages, it is only logical that geographers and linguists have sought to impose some general framework for studying their evolution.

Most textbooks recognize about a dozen language families worldwide. English, the language in which this book is written, belongs to the Germanic subfamily of the Indo-European language family. Indo-European languages are spoken by more people than those of any other family. Chinese, which belongs to the Sino-Tibetan family, is the single most prevalent language; it is spoken by more than 1 billion people.

As you read this volume and study the maps, you will become acquainted with the other important language families as well as many languages within the major families. You will also learn about the evolution of language, culture and the commanding influence of language throughout the world.

The powerful effect of language on human affairs is unavoidable. Almost anywhere in the world that there is conflict, the warring people are likely to speak different languages. As recently as the past few years, the world has witnessed the power of language (and culture) to both unite and divide people. For example, the citizens of what were East and West Germany are, once again, politically united. This was possible, perhaps inevitable, because they shared a common language and culture. Likewise, the recent disintegration of what was known as the Soviet Union occured because politics could not hold together what culture and language divided. In other regions as well — South Africa, India, the Middle East — differences in language reflect cultures in conflict.

As witnessed throughout history, language and culture cannot be separated; they move and change together. The language maps of the world will likely continue to evolve rapidly, as people migrate and as technology provides access to other cultures. Have a good look, for the pattern is changing as we speak!

Scott E. Morris

A legend lists and explains the symbols and colors used on the map. It is called a legend because it tells the story of a map. It is important to read the map legend to find out exactly what the symbols mean because some symbols do not look like what they represent. For example, a dot stands for a town.
Every map in this atlas has a legend on it.

This legend lists and explains the colors and symbols used on the map on that page only. The legend on the left, below, shows examples of the colors used on the maps in all the atlases in this series. Below this is a list of all symbols used on the maps in all the atlases in this series.
The legend on the right, below, is an example of a legend used in the physical atlas.

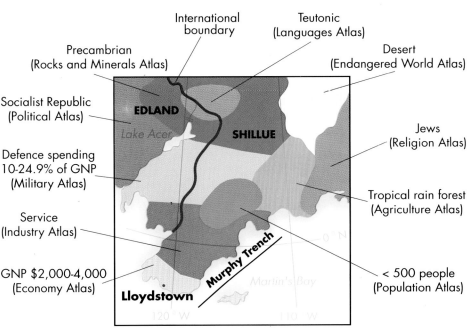

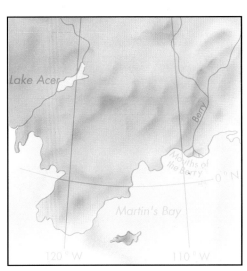

Rocks and Minerals

★	Earthquake	(Fe)	Iron	
▲	Volcano	(Pb)	Lead	
⊤	Coal	(Mn)	Manganese	
	Natural gas	(Pt)	Platinum	
	Oil	(Ag)	Silver	
▽	Diamond	(S)	Sulfur	
(U)	Uranium	(Sn)	Tin	
(Al)	Bauxite	(Ti)	Titanium	
(Cu)	Copper	(Zn)	Zinc	
(Au)	Gold			

Languages

	African Tribal Languages	◊	Indian
★	Creole	◊	Caucasian
	Aborigine	■	Dravidian
—	Basque		
✚	Swahili	●	Kurdish

Religion

★ Important religious place

Endangered World

🧍	Human Pressure	🐄	Animals at Risk
🐘	Animal Pressure	🦅	Birds at Risk
💧	Acid Rain		

Industry

	Oil Refining		Food and Drink
⊛	Hydroelectric Power		Heavy Industry
☢	Nuclear Power		Chemical
	Ship		Textile
✈	Aircraft	🔧	Metal
🚂	Train		Light Industry
🚗	Car		Plastic

Economy

💵	1 Bundle = $1 Billion	🪙	1 Coin = $10 Billion
🪙	1 Coin = $500 Million	🏛	World's Largest Stock Exchanges

Physical

▲	Mountain Peak		Canal

Agriculture and Vegetation

	Wheat		Grapes
	Barley		Fruit
	Maize		Timber
0	Rice		Tobacco
ᴜᴄ	Oats		Coconuts
	Cocoa	▽	Rubber
	Cotton		Cattle
	Silk		Sheep
Y	Sugar		Olives
	Coffee		Soybeans
	Tea	O	Potatoes
	Palm Oil		

Military

	Number of armed forces per 1,000 population		Member of NATO

Political

	Number of Political Parties	★	Capital City

This page is a physical map of the world. It indicates where the major physical features — such as mountain ranges, plains, deserts, lakes, and rivers — are in the world. As the world is very large, the map has to be drawn at a very small scale in order to fit onto a page. This map is drawn at a scale so that 1 inch on the map, at the equator, equals 1,840 miles on the ground.

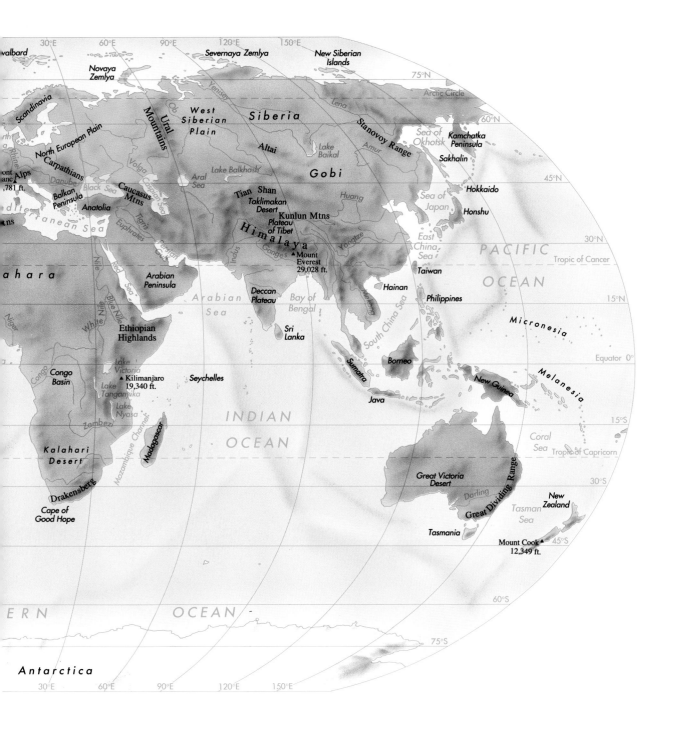

valbard

Novaya
Zemlya

Severnaya Zemlya

New Siberian
Islands

75°N

Scandinavia

Arctic Circle

orth

North European Plain

Ob

Yenisey

West
Siberian
Plain

Siberia

Lena

Stanovoy Range

Sea of
Okhotsk

Kamchatka
Peninsula

60°N

Rhine

Carpathians

Ural
Mountains

Altai

Lake
Baikal

Amur

Sakhalin

anc Alps
781 ft.

Danube

Volga

Caspian Sea

Aral
Sea

Lake Balkhash

Gobi

Huang

45°N

Sea of
Japan

Hokkaido

Balkan
Peninsula

Black Sea

Caucasus
Mtns

Tian Shan

Taklimakan
Desert

Kunlun Mtns

Honshu

ns

Anatolia

Tigris

Euphrates

Plateau
of Tibet

Yangtze

East
China
Sea

PACIFIC

30°N

Himalaya

Persian Gulf

Indus

Ganges

▲Mount
Everest
29,028 ft.

Tropic of Cancer

terranean Sea

ahara

Nile

Red Sea

Arabian
Peninsula

Arabian
Sea

Deccan
Plateau

Bay of
Bengal

Taiwan

OCEAN

Hainan

Philippines

15°N

Niger

Blue Nile

White Nile

Ethiopian
Highlands

Sri
Lanka

South China Sea

Mekong

Micronesia

Congo

Congo
Basin

Lake
Victoria

▲Kilimanjaro
19,340 ft.

Seychelles

Sumatra

Borneo

Equator 0°

Lake
Tanganyika

Java

New Guinea

Melanesia

Lake
Nyasa

Zambezi

INDIAN

15°S

Kalahari
Desert

Mozambique Channel

Madagascar

OCEAN

Coral
Sea

Tropic of Capricorn

Drakensberg

Great Victoria
Desert

Great Dividing Range

30°S

Cape of
Good Hope

Darling

New
Zealand

Great Dividing Range

Tasman
Sea

Tasmania

Mount Cook▲
12,349 ft.

45°S

60°S

ERN

OCEAN

75°S

Antarctica

30°E

60°E

90°E

120°E

150°E

World Key Map

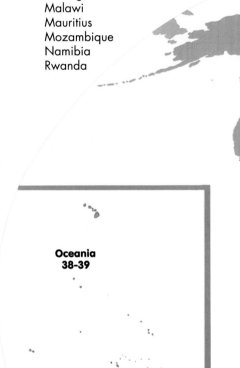

Africa, Northern 10-11

Algeria
Benin
Burkina Faso
Cameroon
Cape Verde
Central African Republic
Chad
Djibouti
Egypt
Ethiopia
Gambia
Ghana
Guinea
Guinea-Bissau
Ivory Coast
Liberia
Libya
Mali
Mauritania
Morocco
Niger
Nigeria
Senegal
Sierra Leone
Somalia
Sudan
Togo
Tunisia
Western Sahara

Africa, Southern 12-13

Angola
Botswana
Burundi
Comoros
Congo
Equatorial Guinea
Gabon
Kenya
Lesotho
Madagascar
Malawi
Mauritius
Mozambique
Namibia
Rwanda

São Tomé & Príncipe
Seychelles
South Africa
Swaziland
Tanzania
Uganda
Zaire
Zambia
Zimbabwe

America, Central 14-15

Antigua & Barbuda
Bahamas
Barbados
Belize
Costa Rica
Cuba
Dominica

Dominican Republic
El Salvador
Grenada
Guatemala
Haiti
Honduras
Jamaica

Mexico
Nicaragua
Panama
St Kitts - Nevis
St Lucia
St Vincent
Trinidad & Tobago

Canada 26-27

Canada

Commonwealth of Independent States 28-29

Armenia
Azerbaijan
Estonia
Georgia
Kazakhstan
Kirghizstan
Latvia
Lithuania
Moldova
Russian Federation

Tajikistan
Turkmenistan
Ukraine
Uzbekhistan

Europe 30-31

Albania
Bosnia & Herzegovina
Bulgaria
Croatia
Czechoslovakia
Finland
Greece
Hungary
Iceland
Norway

Poland
Romania
Slovenia
Sweden
Yugoslavia

Europe, Western 32-33

Andorra
Austria
Belgium
Denmark
France
Germany
Ireland
Italy
Liechtenstein
Luxembourg

Malta
Monaco
Netherlands
Portugal
San Marino
Spain
Switzerland
United Kingdom
Vatican City

America, South 16-17

Argentina	Guyana
Bolivia	Paraguay
Brazil	Peru
Chile	Suriname
Colombia	Uruguay
Ecuador	Venezuela
French Guiana	

Antarctica 18-19

Antarctica

Asia, East 20-21

China
Japan
Korea, North
Korea, South
Mongolia
Taiwan

Asia, Southeast 22-23

Brunei
Burma
Cambodia
Indonesia
Laos
Malaysia
Philippines
Singapore
Thailand
Vietnam

Australasia 24-25

Australia
New Zealand
Papua New Guinea

Europe 30-31

Western Europe 32-33

Commonwealth of Independent States 28-29

Northern Africa 10-11

Middle East 36-37

East Asia 20-21

Indian Subcontinent 34-35

Southern Africa 12-13

Southeast Asia 22-23

Oceania 38-39

Australasia 24-25

Antarctica 18-19

United States of America 40-41

United States of America

Indian Subcontinent 34-35

Afghanistan
Bangladesh
Bhutan
India
Maldives
Nepal
Pakistan
Sri Lanka

Middle East 36-37

Bahrain	Saudi Arabia
Cyprus	Syria
Iran	Turkey
Iraq	United Arab Emirates
Israel	Yemen
Jordan	
Kuwait	
Lebanon	
Oman	
Qatar	

Oceania 38-39

Fiji
Kiribati
Nauru
Solomon Islands
Tonga
Tuvalu
Vanuatu
Western Samoa

Many of the great civilizations, including ancient Egyptian, Greek, Roman, Ottoman, and European, have each left their mark on North Africa. French, English, Italian and Spanish — as well as Arabic and tribal languages — are all spoken in the region.

How Do We Communicate ?

People send each other messages in many ways. This is called communication. Sometimes people use movements of their body, or they use words. People also use sounds or signs.
A cat can show happiness by purring, or anger by arching its back. People use sounds and movements just like cats. These movements are called body language. This can be confusing, because a shout can mean anger or that someone is hurt. Words give a clearer, fuller message. The growth of whole groups of words or languages helped people to pass on ideas and messages.

What the colors and symbols mean

Semitic and Hemitic

Romance (French, Italian, Spanish,etc)

EDLAND

SHILLUE

0°N

Martin's Bay

120°W   110°W

Teutonic (English, German,etc)

Uninhabited African Land

★ Creole

🐟 African Tribal Languages

0   200   400   600 miles

African Languages

In North Africa, Semitic languages are spoken, and dialects of Arabic are used in Egypt and along the Mediterranean Coast.
The Berbers have their own language, while in Ethiopia there are over 80 different languages spoken, though few are written down.

❓ Did You Know

★ Over a thousand languages are spoken in Africa.

★ African tribes used drum beats to send their messages.

How many can read ?

A selection of countries in Northern Africa.

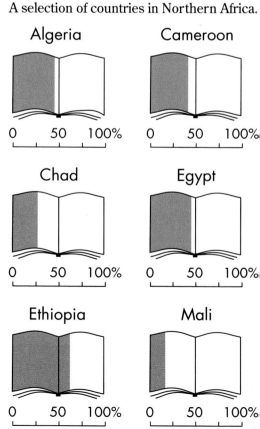

Algeria

0   50   100%

Cameroon

0   50   100%

Chad

0   50   100%

Egypt

0   50   100%

Ethiopia

0   50   100%

Mali

0   50   100%

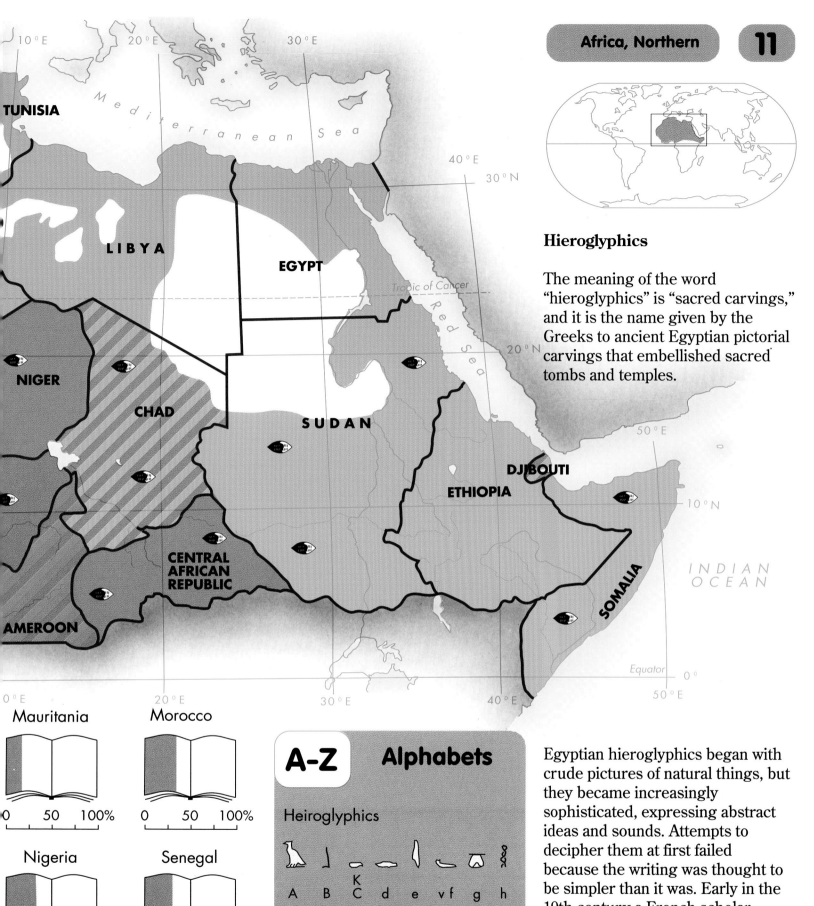

TUNISIA

Mediterranean Sea

10°E   20°E   30°E   40°E   30°N

LIBYA

EGYPT

Tropic of Cancer

Red Sea   20°N

NIGER

CHAD

SUDAN   50°E

DJIBOUTI

ETHIOPIA   10°N

CENTRAL
AFRICAN
REPUBLIC

SOMALIA   *INDIAN
OCEAN*

AMEROON

Equator   0°

0°E   20°E   30°E   40°E   50°E

Hieroglyphics

The meaning of the word "hieroglyphics" is "sacred carvings," and it is the name given by the Greeks to ancient Egyptian pictorial carvings that embellished sacred tombs and temples.

Mauritania | Morocco

0   50   100%   0   50   100%

Nigeria | Senegal

0   50   100%   0   50   100%

Sudan | Tunisia

0   50   100%   0   50   100%

A-Z **Alphabets**

Heiroglyphics

A B C(K) d e vf g h

i l m N o P q

R S SA T U.W y ch sh

j u KH TH fish life man woman

Egyptian hieroglyphics began with crude pictures of natural things, but they became increasingly sophisticated, expressing abstract ideas and sounds. Attempts to decipher them at first failed because the writing was thought to be simpler than it was. Early in the 19th century a French scholar, Champollion, examined a piece of broken black stone found in Egypt; covered in three kinds of writing–hieroglyphics, "people's script," and Greek– this valuable find is known as the Rosetta stone. From this, he managed to translate the language of hieroglyphics and so release the secrets of ancient Egypt to the world.

Colonized mainly by the English and Dutch, southern Africans speak those languages plus many native African tongues. Other European languages include French, German, Spanish, and Italian.

Amazing – But True

★ There are a group of languages in South-West Africa known as click languages because of their distinctive click sound, like the noise you use to encourage a horse to move on, which is written as an X.

Tracking

Tracking signs were once an important way of passing on information in areas that were unexplored. They are still used today by American Indians.

African Languages

Bantu is the main family of languages spoken in Africa south of the Sahara. There are over 300 Bantu languages. One of the best known is Swahili, because although only about a million people use it as their mother tongue, it is a common language used by over 10 million people in East Africa.

Most Bantu languages were not written down until the 19th century, and the Arabic script was borrowed from Arabs trading along the east coast of Africa and used for Swahili. Elsewhere the Roman alphabet, with additional characters, has been used.

West African languages are tonal; some have as many as four distinct tones for the same word, each having a different meaning. Another interesting feature is that some languages don't distinguish between past, present and future tense, but just refer to completed and uncompleted actions. Hausa and Fula are rich languages with much religious poetry written in an Arabic script.

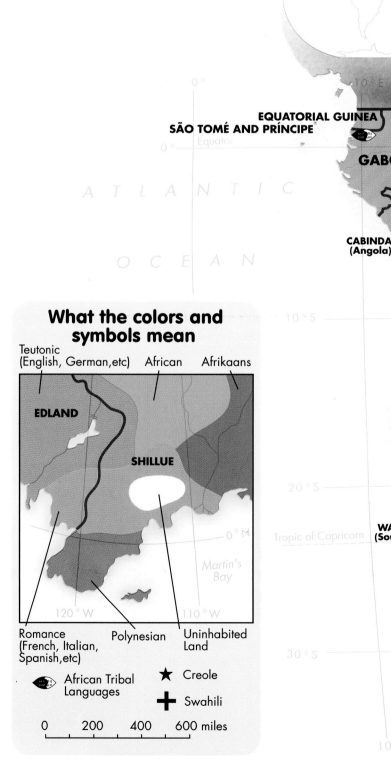

What the colors and symbols mean

Teutonic (English, German, etc)   African   Afrikaans

EDLAND

SHILLUE

Romance (French, Italian, Spanish, etc)   Polynesian   Uninhabited Land

African Tribal Languages   ★ Creole

+ Swahili

0   200   400   600 miles

EQUATORIAL GUINEA
SÃO TOMÉ AND PRÍNCIPE
Equator
GABON   CONGO
CABINDA (Angola)
ANGOLA
NAMIBIA
WALVIS BAY (South Africa)
Tropic of Capricorn
SOUT

ATLANTIC

OCEAN

Try laying a trail yourself with the help of some friends. Two people go first and lay out the trail. Make the signs out of sticks and stones and other natural objects. Leave as many signs as possible to make it more fun. After a while, the others set off to follow the trail and try and find the first two.

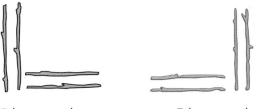

Take next path to the right

Take next path to the left

Go uphill

Go downhill

Follow arrow

Dead end — go back to beginning of trail

How many can read ?

A selection of countries in southern Africa.

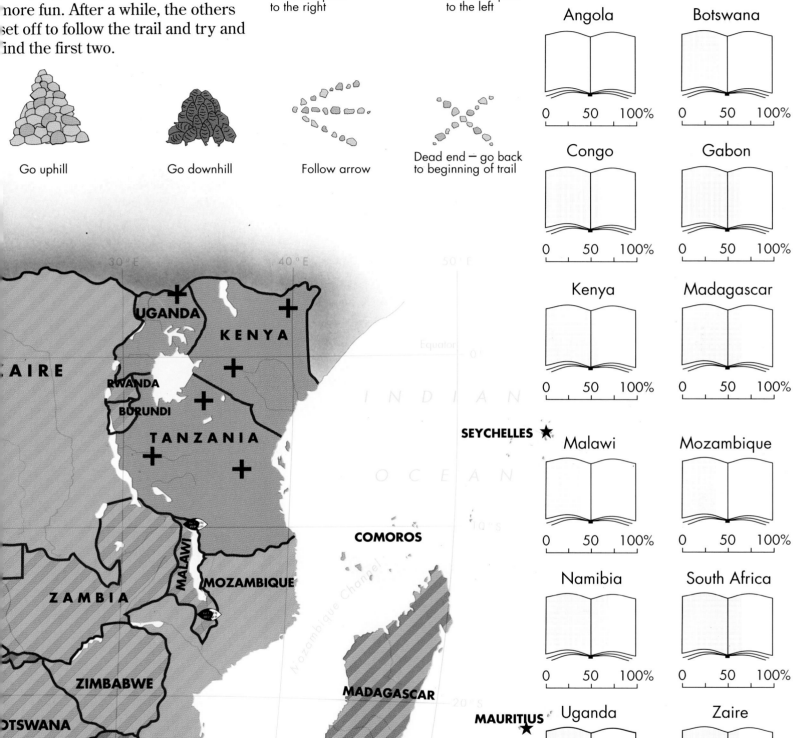

Angola
0   50   100%

Botswana
0   50   100%

Congo
0   50   100%

Gabon
0   50   100%

Kenya
0   50   100%

Madagascar
0   50   100%

Malawi
0   50   100%

Mozambique
0   50   100%

Namibia
0   50   100%

South Africa
0   50   100%

Uganda
0   50   100%

Zaire
0   50   100%

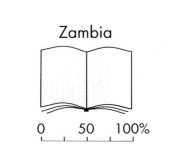

Zambia
0   50   100%

The most important language in the area is Spanish, spoken by almost all peoples and brought by Spanish conquerors in the 16th century. Most native languages died out when the populations were killed by the diseases and warfare the invaders brought with them.

The Development of Languages

Long ago it could take many weeks for a message to travel from one place to another. Now it is possible to pick up a telephone and talk to that person although they are a long distance away. Sometimes people learn other languages so that they can understand other people from different countries. Early languages probably grew in much the same way as babies learn to talk. First there were cries and sounds that were copied. Next came words for things, people or animals. We have to guess how languages developed as we know very little about the first languages, which were not written down.

? Did You Know

★ In Central America Mayan is the most important family of languages, spoken in Mexico, Honduras, and Guatemala. It is the only American Indian language with an ancient alphabet.

★ An amazing number of different languages, over 1,000, are spoken by American Indians. The remarkable thing is that these often differ as much from one another as English differs from Chinese.

International Languages

The idea of an artificially constructed language that would be understood by everyone dates back to the 17th century, when Latin was no longer the language of scholarship. Esperanto, launched in 1887, was one of the most popular attempts and gained wide support. There have been many different attempts to get a common means of communication, and one of the more recent ones has been looking at "linguistic universals," features that are common to all languages, in the quest for an ideal language.

How many can read ?

Antigua and Barbuda
50   100%

Bahamas
0   50   100%

Dominica
0   50   100%

Dominican Republic
0   50   100%

Honduras
0   50   100%

Jamaica
0   50   100%

Barbados
50   100%

Belize
0   50   100%

El Salvador
0   50   100%

Grenada
0   50   100%

Mexico
0   50   100%

Nicaragua
0   50   100%

Costa Rica
50   100%

Cuba
0   50   100%

Guatemala
0   50   100%

Haiti
0   50   100%

Panama
0   50   100%

St. Kitts - Nevis
0   50   100%

St. Lucia
0   50   100%

St. Vincent
0   50   100%

Trinidad and Tobago
0   50   100%

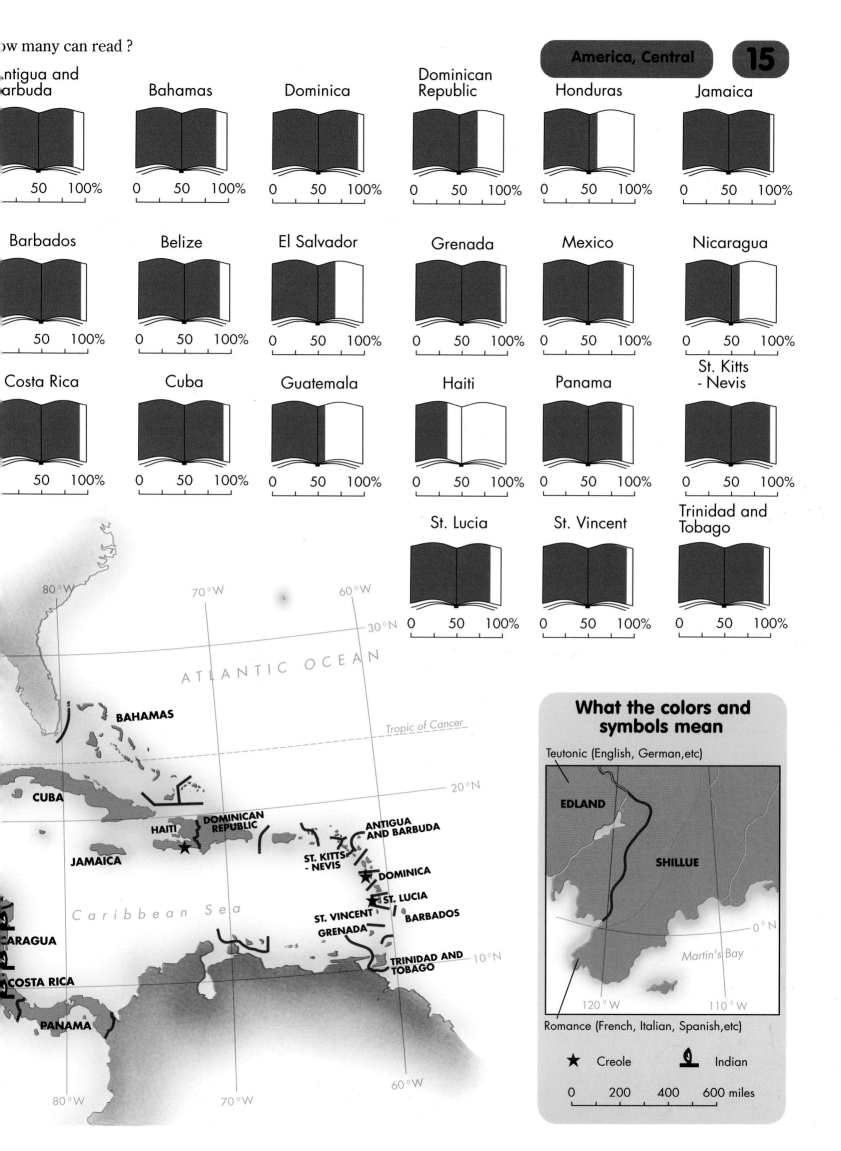

80°W   70°W   60°W

30°N

ATLANTIC OCEAN

BAHAMAS

Tropic of Cancer

20°N

CUBA

DOMINICAN REPUBLIC

HAITI

ANTIGUA AND BARBUDA

ST. KITTS - NEVIS

DOMINICA

JAMAICA

ST. LUCIA

Caribbean Sea

ST. VINCENT

BARBADOS

GRENADA

NICARAGUA

TRINIDAD AND TOBAGO   10°N

COSTA RICA

PANAMA

80°W   70°W

60°W

What the colors and symbols mean

Teutonic (English, German, etc)

EDLAND

SHILLUE

0°N

Martin's Bay

120°W   110°W

Romance (French, Italian, Spanish, etc)

★ Creole   🕯 Indian

0   200   400   600 miles

This continent is dominated by Hispanic speakers — a result of Spanish and Portuguese colonization of the 15th and 16th centuries. Some native languages do survive. The ancient Inca language, Quechua, was never written — only spoken.

South American Languages

In South America there are many families of languages. The largest are the Arawak, the Carib, the Chibcha and the Tupi-Guarani families. Quechua is of particular interest because it is the language of the Incas and it is still one of the recognized languages of Peru, Bolivia and Ecuador.

Spanish and Portugese Languages

Spanish is spoken by over 200 million people, 38 million in Spain and the rest mostly in South and Central America. It is the fourth most popular language after Chinese, English, and Hindi. The standard language of Spain is Castilian, and in sound it is quite like Italian. It has a strong "r" sound, a sound like the Scottish "ch" (written as "j" or "g"). As in many European languages, nouns are either masculine or feminine. Many of the masculine words end in "o" and the feminine in "a." Spelling in Spanish is simple as most letters correspond to one sound only.
Portuguese is spoken by about 10 million people in Portugal and over 135 million in Brazil. Forms of it are used in many other areas, including Africa, India, and parts of Asia. It has many sounds that are not in Spanish, including nasal vowels.

How many can read ?

A selection of countries in South America.

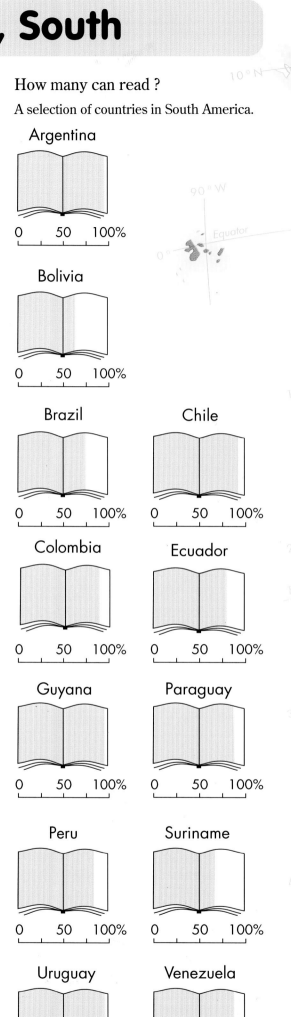

Argentina
0   50   100%

Bolivia
0   50   100%

Brazil
0   50   100%

Chile
0   50   100%

Colombia
0   50   100%

Ecuador
0   50   100%

Guyana
0   50   100%

Paraguay
0   50   100%

Peru
0   50   100%

Suriname
0   50   100%

Uruguay
0   50   100%

Venezuela
0   50   100%

Indian Sign Language

Indian tribes speak many different languages and therefore need some way of communicating with each other.

Trade Friend Peace

A form of sign language developed out of simple gestures, enabling the Indians to understand each other. This language is not complete, and it cannot express complicated ideas.

What the colors and symbols mean

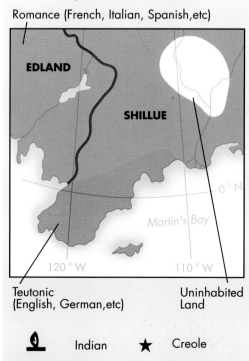

Romance (French, Italian, Spanish, etc)

EDLAND

SHILLUE

Martin's Bay

Teutonic (English, German, etc) Uninhabited Land

Indian ★ Creole

0 200 400 600 miles

![Amazing - But True]

! Amazing – But True

★ In days gone by Incas from Peru used 'quipos,' knotted wools of different lengths and thicknesses, as a way of keeping records.

Uninhabited and unexplored until recent times, Antarctica has no language of its own. Since the beginning of the 20th century, however, an increasing number of nations have laid claim to territories on this bleak and frozen continent, because of the rich natural resources available. The British, French, Russians, Argentinians, Japanese, and Australians all maintain research stations there.

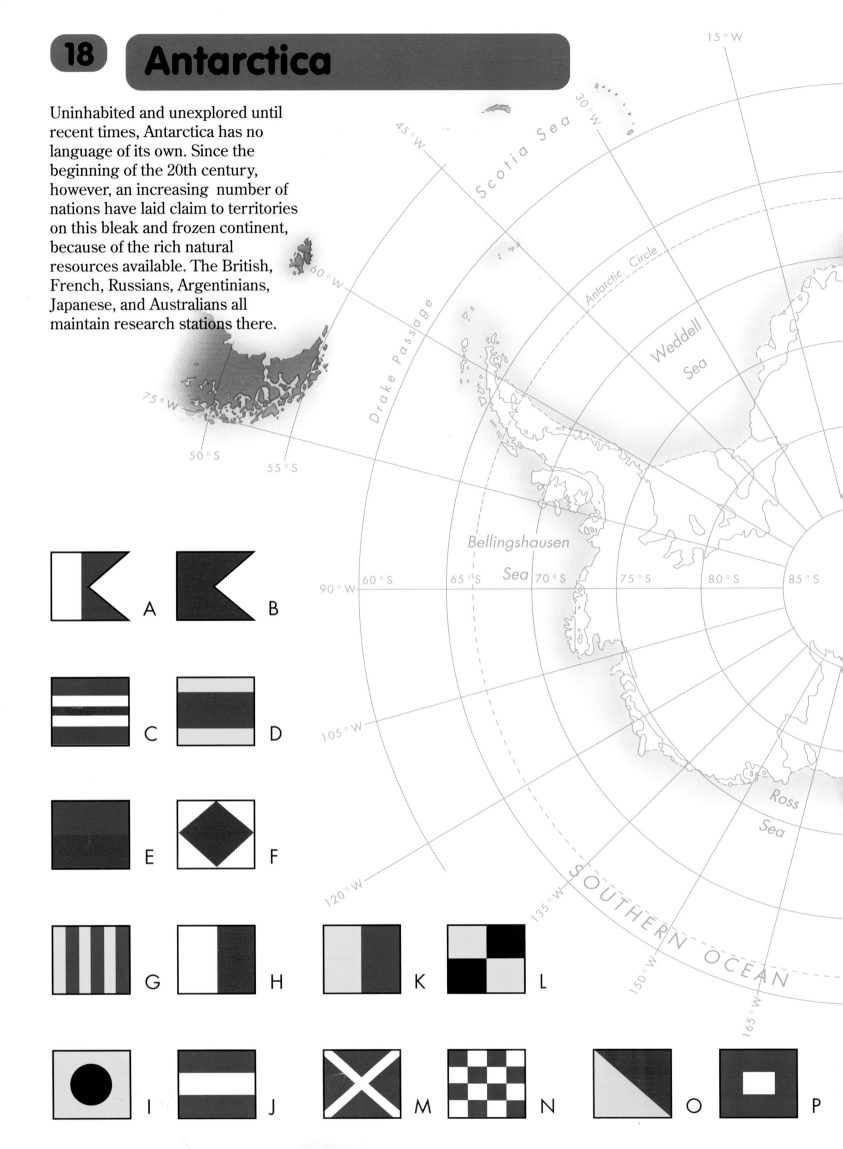

A   B

C   D

E   F

G   H   K   L

I   J   M   N   O   P

International Flag Code

Flags are a useful way of sending messages. They are particularly important for communicating at sea, and there is an international flag code which ships can use to send messages.

There are square flags for each letter of the alphabet and triangular pennants for the numbers 0–9. When signaling, sailors hoist groups of between one and five flags. Many flags or groups of flags have special meanings.

For example, a ship that is about to leave port hoists the flag for P, commonly called the Blue Peter; RY means "My crew has mutinied"; NC means "I am in distress and need immediate help"; and AD means "I must abandon ship." Nowadays ships communicate by radio, but flags are still a good way of sending messages over short distances. The international flag code is also very useful for ships in foreign waters where the captain may want to signal to someone who does not speak the same language. The international flag code explains the code in nine languages.

They are English, French, German, Greek, Italian, Japanese, Norwegian, Russian, and Spanish.

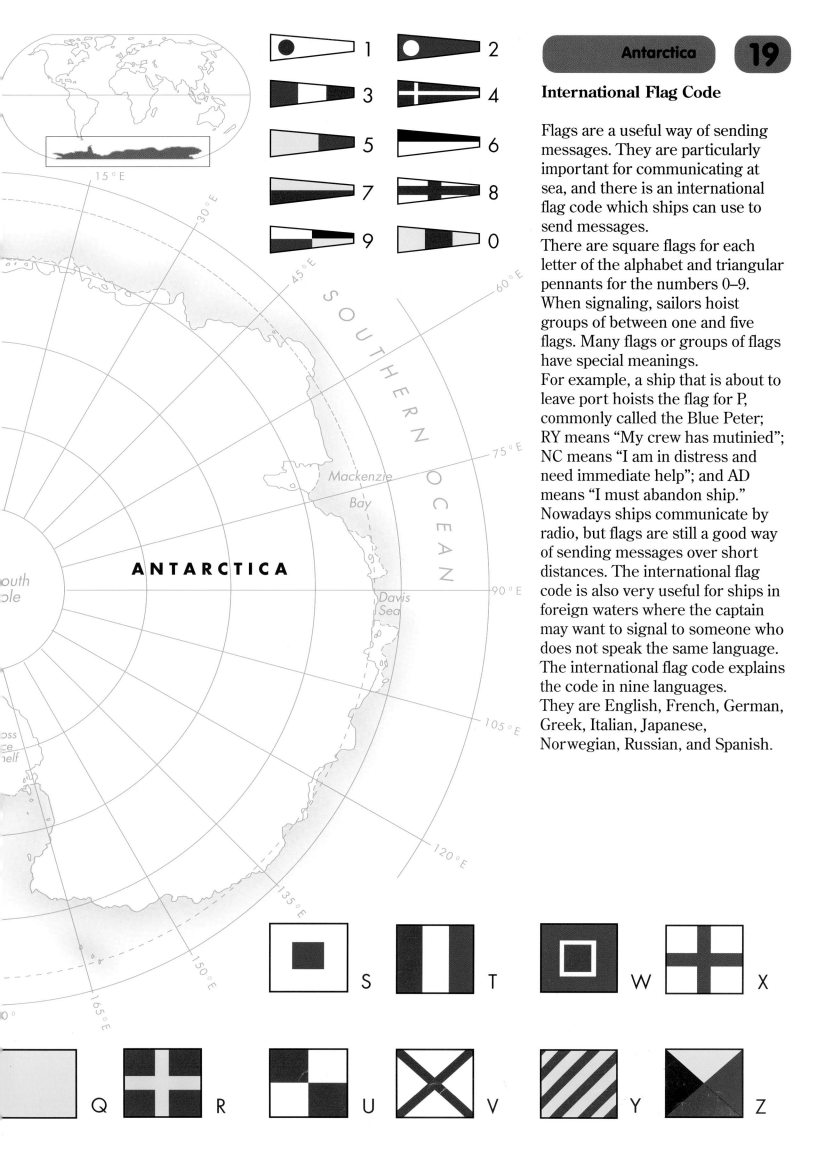

SOUTHERN OCEAN

ANTARCTICA

Mackenzie Bay

Davis Sea

South Pole

Ross Ice Shelf

15°E
30°E
45°E
60°E
75°E
90°E
105°E
120°E
135°E
150°E
165°E
0°

1 • 2 ○ 3 4 5 6 7 8 9 0

S T W X

Q R U V Y Z

As the most populous country in the world, China and its languages dominate East Asia. Chinese is a complex language that has up to 20 million characters.

Chinese Language

Writing in the West is phonetic, with letters or groups of letters representing sounds. Therefore, we depend on sound alone for the meaning of a word whether we are writing, reading or speaking.
In Chinese, each word is represented by a word-picture or "character" that is pronounced differently in different dialects but has the same meaning. Therefore, the spoken words differ in different Chinese dialects, and people can only communicate in the written language.
This is gradually changing. There is now a standard form of Chinese, based on the northern dialect, that is being developed as a national language.
Since 1949 the Government of China has made great efforts to simplify the language and to teach everyone to read. Now only 1,500 basic characters are needed to read a newspaper. Books used to be arranged in vertical columns and read from left to right; now they are usually composed horizontally like Western books.
Learning Chinese is further complicated for the Westerner by the fact that it is a tonal language. The same syllable means different things when pronounced with different inflecions of the voice. The syllable t'u (pronounced "two") means "bald" in one tone, "disciple" in a second, "earth" in a third, and "rabbit" in a fourth.

Making Paper

Paper was invented in China in AD 105 by Cai Lun. He used the inner bark of a tree for fiber. Paper gets its name from papyrus, a reed used by the ancient Egyptians for making writing material. Today paper is made from wood pulp, but you can make your own recycled paper.

2. Add 2 teaspoons of instant starch and fill the bowl with warm water. Leave for 10 minutes. Next beat it with a fork until it is all mixed.

3. Dip a piece of fine wire gauze, about 6 inches square, edge first into the bowl. Lift it out flat and let the water drip out. Gently turn the gauze onto a piece of absorbent paper.

1. Tear up used paper into tiny pieces and place them in a bowl.

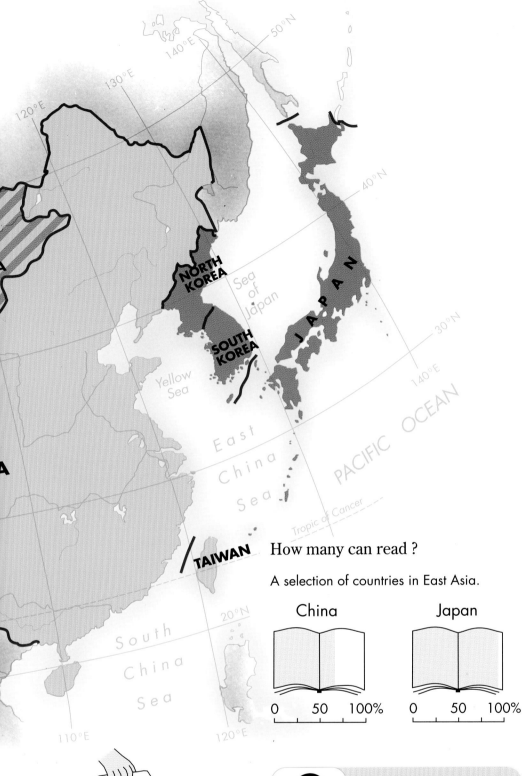

How many can read ?

A selection of countries in East Asia.

China

Japan

0 50 100%   0 50 100%

Japanese Language

Japanese and Chinese are not related languages, though Japanese has borrowed a great number of words from Chinese since ancient times. Japanese script is an adaptation of the Chinese system, written in vertical columns from right to left. Because the system is pictorial, Japanese can disregard the sounds of the characters and use them to write their own words — much as the number 3 is used in many different languages.

The Japanese sound system is very different from that of English. No word or syllable can end in a consonant (except "n"). There is no "l" sound. It has no genders or articles (a or the) and no number in nouns or verbs. "Hito" means "man" or "men," and "Kau" means "I" "you," "he," "she," "we" or "they."

Attempts have been made to simplify the language and limit the number of characters in common use to 1,950. Children in primary school are taught about 880.

4. Ask an adult to iron the blotting paper until it is dry. Peel off the top piece of absorbent paper slowly to see your sheet of handmade paper. Leave it to dry for a day.

5. Remove the gauze leaving the pulp behind and cover with another piece of absorbent paper. Press firmly using a rolling pin.

? Did You Know

★ The earliest written language was discovered on Yangshao culture pottery near Xi'an (Sian) in China — dated 5000-4000 BC.

★ In East Asia Chinese writing is considered an art; it has 40,000 characters compared with the English alphabet of 26 letters. Some characters take as many as 32 strokes of the pen to write.

What the colors and symbols mean

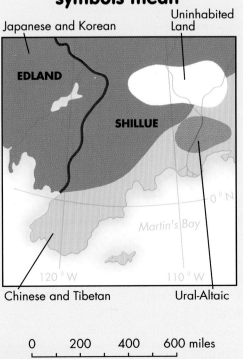

Japanese and Korean

Uninhabited Land

EDLAND

SHILLUE

Martin's Bay

Chinese and Tibetan

Ural-Altaic

0 200 400 600 miles

How many can read?

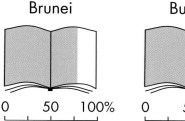

0   50   100%   0   50   100%

Most of the peoples of Southeast Asia speak one or more Indonesian languages, largely drawn from Malayan, but including words from English, Dutch, and Arabic. English is a compulsorily taught second language.

Semaphore

Semaphore

Semaphore is another way of using flags to send messages. The sender holds two flags, one in each hand. The position in which he puts them indicates a letter of the alphabet. When he comes to the end of a word he holds the flags crossed in front of him, and the receiver knows that the next letter signaled is the first letter of the next word. The first semaphore signals did not actually use flags but were made by placing mechanical arms in different positions. This early semaphore system was invented by Claude Chappe, a French engineer, in 1793. He wanted to find a way of sending messages quickly from Paris to other European cities. He built a string of towers on high ground. On top of each tower was a mast with two mechanical arms. The position of these arms could be changed from the ground by a series of winches. During the day someone with a telescope would keep a lookout, and when they saw a message on a tower in the distance, they would read it and pass it on to the next tower down the line. When the electric telegraph was invented semaphore towers were no longer used, but people were already adapting the invention for their own needs. Railroad engineers used the idea of semaphore code, which was developed using flags. Even today this code is an important way of sending messages when ships have to keep radio silence.

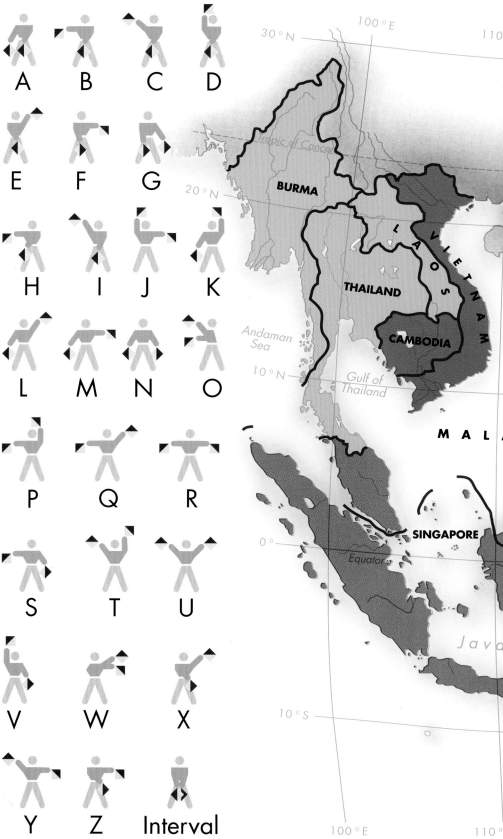

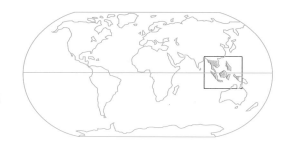

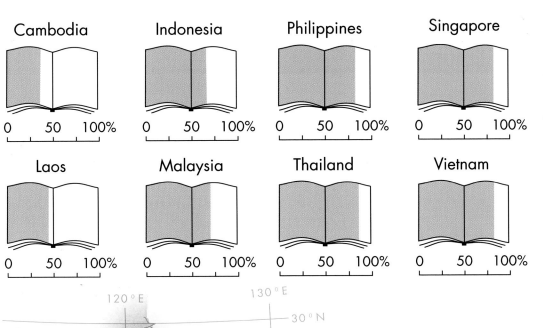

Cambodia	Indonesia	Philippines	Singapore
0 50 100%	0 50 100%	0 50 100%	0 50 100%

Laos	Malaysia	Thailand	Vietnam
0 50 100%	0 50 100%	0 50 100%	0 50 100%

Indonesian Languages

The commonest Indonesian language is Malay, which is spoken by nearly all the inhabitants of Indonesia, Malaysia, and Singapore (about 120 million people). It is one of the easiest languages in the world to learn. With few rules of grammar and simple pronunciation, meanings are shown by the order and grouping of words. As one learns more, however, one realizes that Malay is so full of subtle shades of meaning that no foreigner could ever really hope to master it.

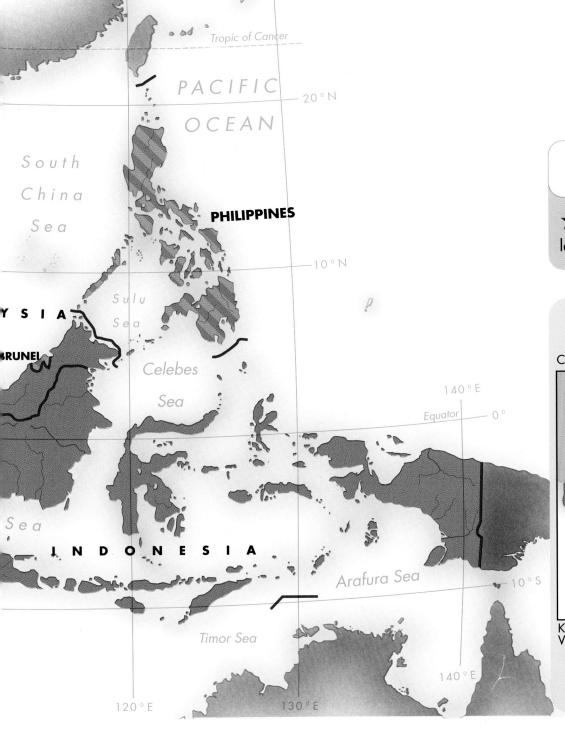

PACIFIC

OCEAN

South
China
Sea

Tropic of Cancer

30°N

20°N

PHILIPPINES

10°N

Sulu
Sea

BRUNEI

Celebes
Sea

140°E

Equator 0°

YSIA

Sea

I N D O N E S I A

Arafura Sea 10°S

Timor Sea

120°E 130°E 140°E

Amazing – But True

★ The language with the most letters is Cambodian, with 72.

What the colors and symbols mean

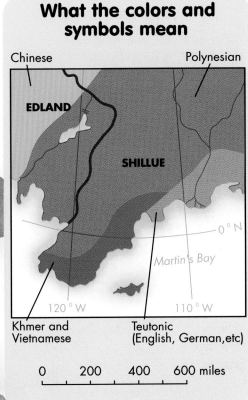

Chinese   Polynesian

EDLAND

SHILLUE

0°N

Martin's Bay

120°W   110°W

Khmer and   Teutonic
Vietnamese   (English, German, etc)

0   200   400   600 miles

Although dominated by an English-speaking population whose ancestors came from Britain, the region also contains a native population, the aborigines, whose language is amongst the oldest on Earth. A wide variety of other languages are spoken by the many island populations.

Use of Symbols

Symbols are a quick and easy means of passing on information, and they are commonly used on all sorts of different items from domestic appliances and clothes to automobile dashboards. They are all simplified designs, which show for example what a push button,

Amazing – But True

★ Australian aborigines make a clicking sound to talk to each other. They also use message sticks — the notches they cut act as a code.

★ Papua New Guinea, owing to its isolated valleys, has the greatest concentration of separate languages in the world with more than 10% of the world total.

What the colors and symbols mean

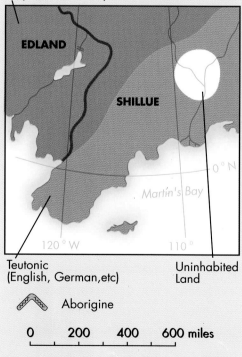

Polynesian and Papua Australian

EDLAND

SHILLUE

Teutonic (English, German, etc)

Uninhabited Land

Aborigine

0   200   400   600 miles

How many can read ?

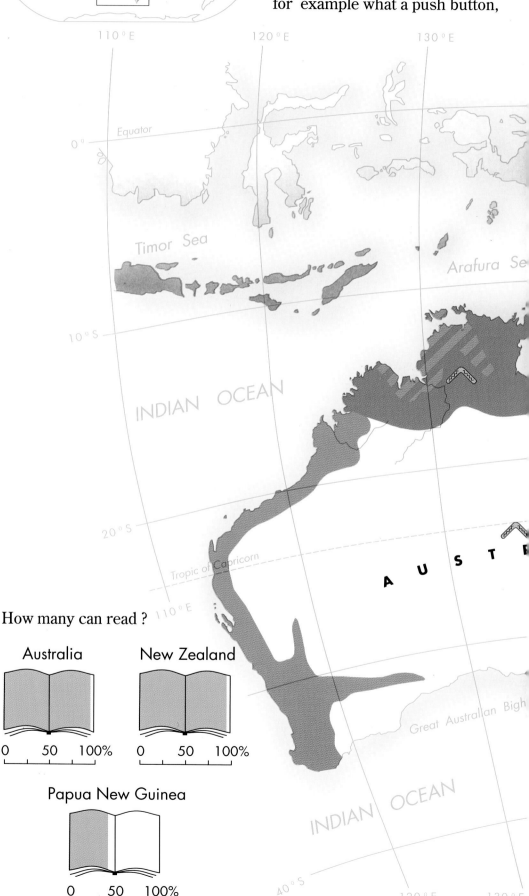

Australia

0   50   100%

New Zealand

0   50   100%

Papua New Guinea

0   50   100%

ever, or handle will do. Symbols are often used to give a warning. Symbols that are used on everyday articles are usually simple and easily understood. The language of symbols is international, a language that is wordless and was devised so that it could be used and understood the whole world over. If, on a washing machine, the words "wash in progress" were written on the panel instead of a symbol, only those who understand English would comprehend the meaning. The same make of washing machine is sold in many countries, so the "language" beside the button has to be something that everyone understands regardless of nationality.

International Road Signs

The universal language of road signs is especially important today on the network of highways that cut across Europe and other continents. Signs tell us how fast we may drive, how far it is to the next gas station; they can warn of fog and of accidents and blockages on the road ahead. We may not be able to speak the language of the country in which we are driving, but we can understand the meaning of many of the road signs.

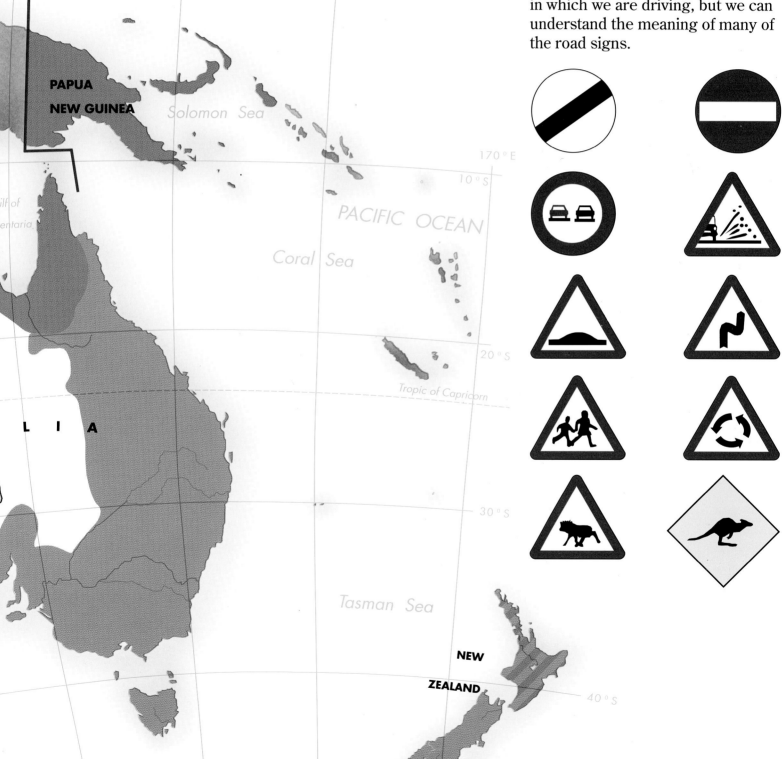

Home of many native North Americans, Canada is also a land of many immigrants from all over the world. Eskimo-Aleut and Algonkian languages were joined first by English and French, then other European and Far Eastern tongues.

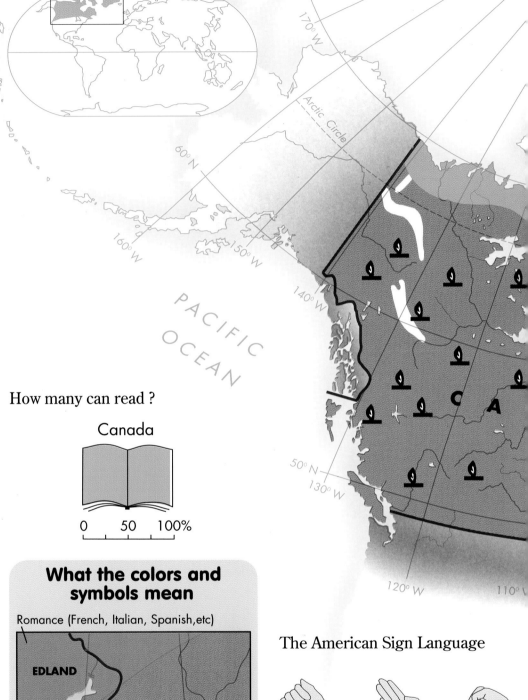

Deaf Communication

Lip reading is one form of deaf communication that is extremely difficult for those who have never heard the sound of words. It is very useful to many people who have gradually lost their hearing. There are about 40 sounds in English speech, each pronounced by a different position of the lips, tongue, and teeth. Each word is made up of two or more sounds. A deaf person has to know the combinations of mouth movements that make up different words. Lip reading is complicated by the fact that so many words look alike. In addition, people do not always speak slowly or use their lips when they speak.

Sign language is another form of deaf communication. It is made up of two parts, the manual alphabet and signs for whole words. Most common words have signs that are made with hand and arm movements done in relation to different parts of the body, and most of these come from natural gestures, such as shivering for cold; or simple mimes. Uncommon words and names are finger spelled using the manual alphabet. Experts are able to communicate almost as quickly as when speaking.

How many can read ?

Canada

0   50   100%

What the colors and symbols mean

Romance (French, Italian, Spanish, etc)

EDLAND

SHILLUE

0° N

Martin's Bay

120° W   110° W

Teutonic (English, German, etc)   Uninhabited Land   Eskimo

Indian

0   200   400   600 miles

The American Sign Language

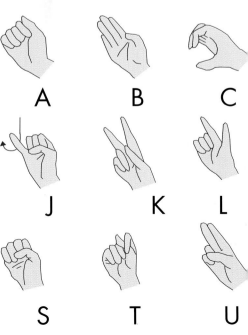

A   B   C

J   K   L

S   T   U

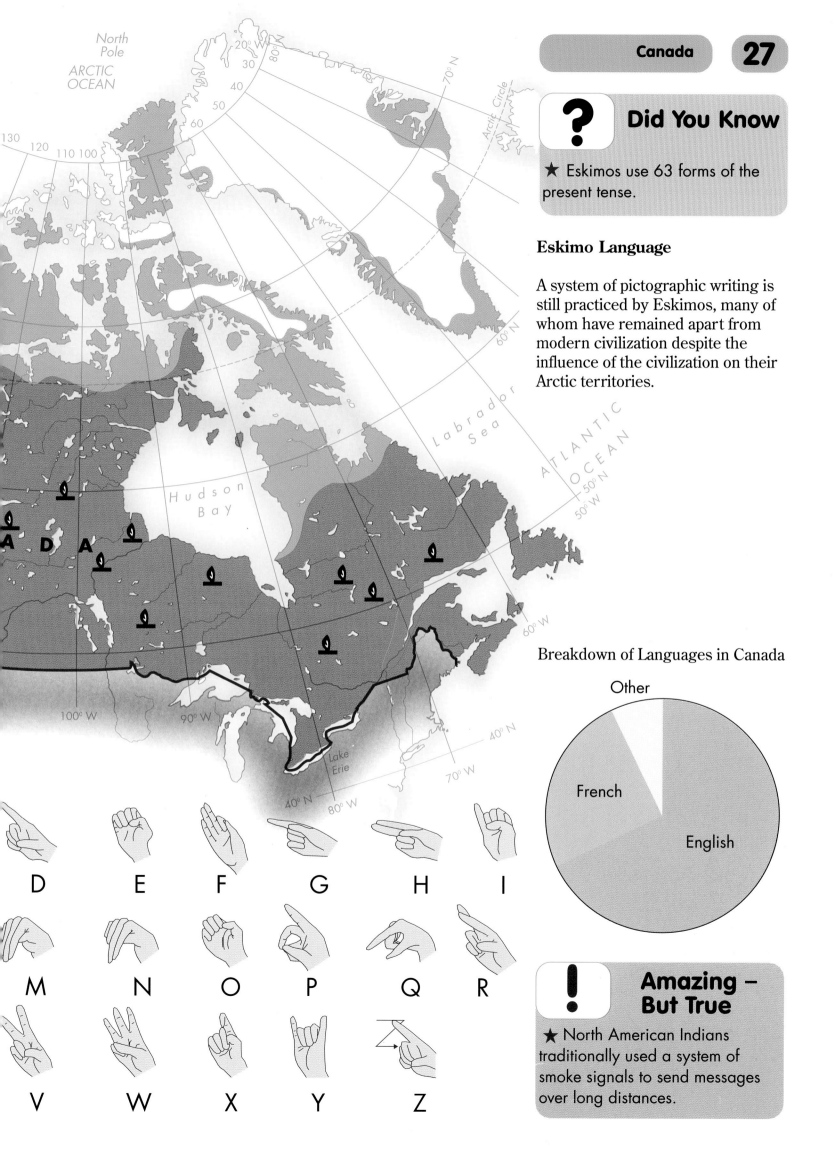

? Did You Know

★ Eskimos use 63 forms of the present tense.

Eskimo Language

A system of pictographic writing is still practiced by Eskimos, many of whom have remained apart from modern civilization despite the influence of the civilization on their Arctic territories.

Breakdown of Languages in Canada

Other

French

English

! Amazing – But True

★ North American Indians traditionally used a system of smoke signals to send messages over long distances.

D E F G H I

M N O P Q R

V W X Y Z

The former Soviet Union includes many countries extending from Europe in the west to the Far East. Although Russian is the official language, the many regional languages reflect a huge cultural, ethnic, and geographic spread.

Slavonic Languages

Well over 200 million people speak Slavonic languages, which include Russian, Polish, Czech, and others. These languages are highly inflected, with many different endings according to the function of the word in the sentence. They have few tenses but make a distinction between actions finished or of limited time and those that are continuous. Changes as well to the final syllables produce subtle changes of meaning. In Russian the name Vaska may also be Vasya or Vasyenka to show changes in the affection of the speaker.

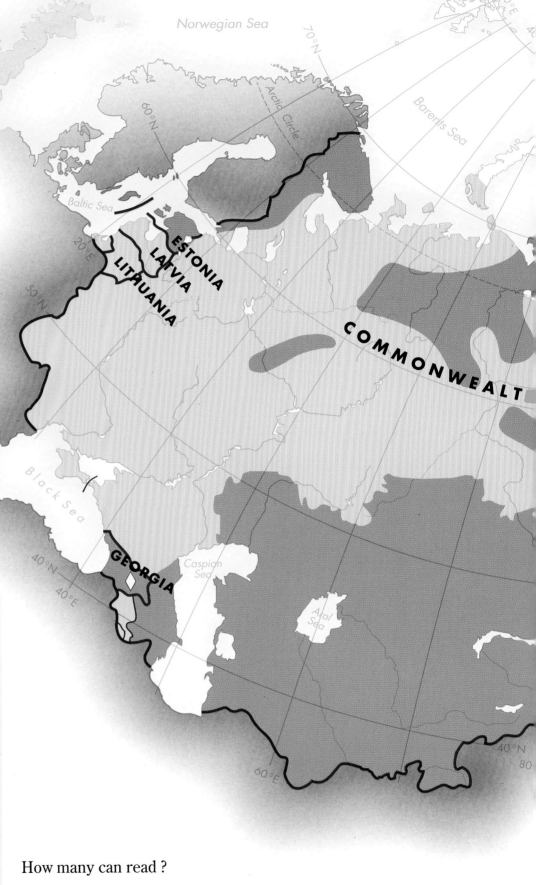

What the colors and symbols mean

Uninhabited Land

Other Indo-European

EDLAND

SHILLUE

Slavic   Eskimo   Ural-Altaic

◇ Caucasian   ★ Creole

0   200   400   600 miles

How many can read ?

CIS

0   50   100%

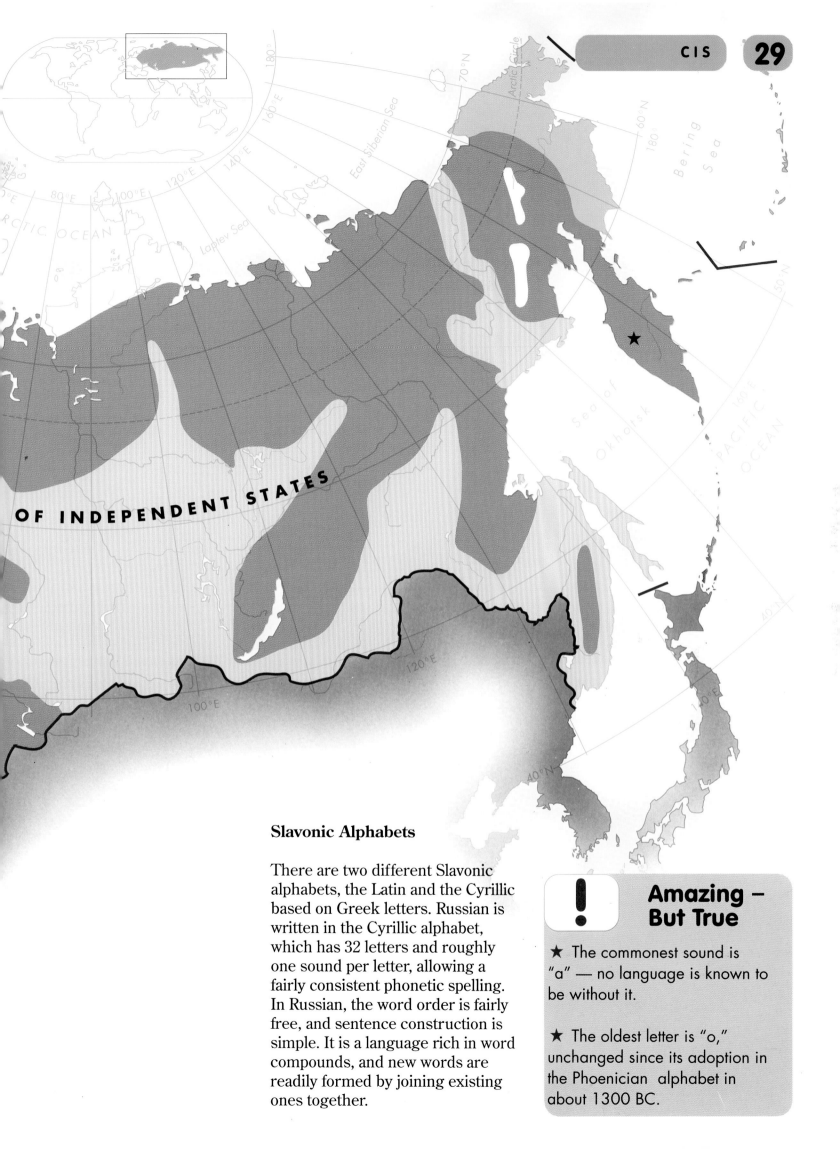

Slavonic Alphabets

There are two different Slavonic alphabets, the Latin and the Cyrillic based on Greek letters. Russian is written in the Cyrillic alphabet, which has 32 letters and roughly one sound per letter, allowing a fairly consistent phonetic spelling. In Russian, the word order is fairly free, and sentence construction is simple. It is a language rich in word compounds, and new words are readily formed by joining existing ones together.

Amazing – But True

★ The commonest sound is "a" — no language is known to be without it.

★ The oldest letter is "o," unchanged since its adoption in the Phoenician alphabet in about 1300 BC.

Most European languages are derived from Latin and Greek or from the Slavonic and Germanic languages, which originated in the East and were brought to Europe when the tribes of eastern Europe and Asia invaded the crumbling Roman Empire.

Scandinavian Languages

Danish, Swedish, and Norwegian are all descended from Old Norse. During the Middle Ages, Danish gradually replaced Norwegian as the upper-class language of Norway, but Norwegian did not die out, and there are now two languages in Norway. Riksmål is really a form of Danish and is the language of literature. The second language is Landsmål, "country language," which was created in the 19th century out of a number of peasant dialects and became widely used.

Finnish and Allied Languages

Finnish, Estonian, Hungarian, and Lappish are a family of languages spoken by many different people from Hungary and Finland to the Lapp regions of northern Scandinavia, Russia, and parts of Siberia and Soviet Asia. These languages have large literatures that date back to medieval times.

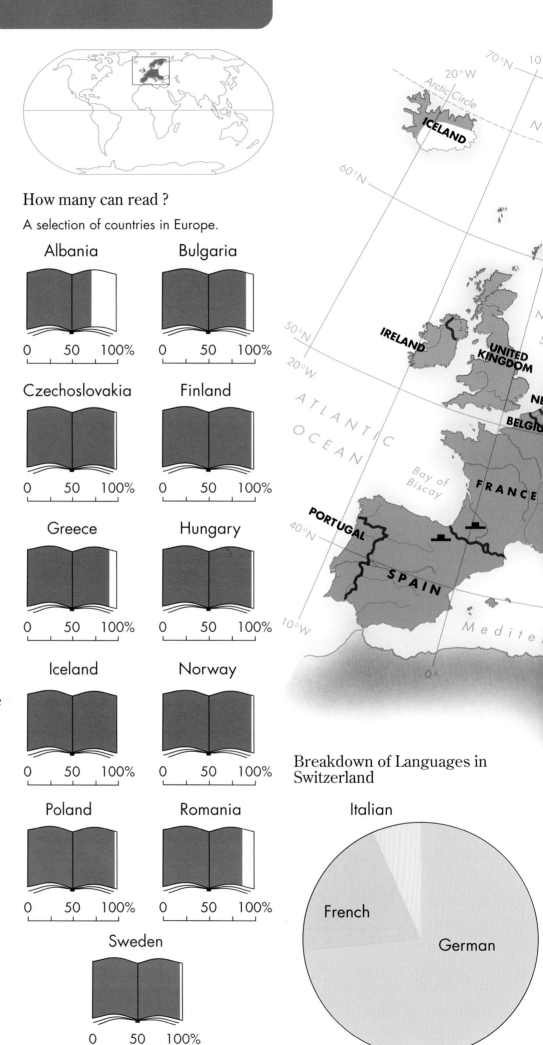

How many can read ?

A selection of countries in Europe.

Albania
0   50   100%

Bulgaria
0   50   100%

Czechoslovakia
0   50   100%

Finland
0   50   100%

Greece
0   50   100%

Hungary
0   50   100%

Iceland
0   50   100%

Norway
0   50   100%

Poland
0   50   100%

Romania
0   50   100%

Sweden
0   50   100%

Breakdown of Languages in Switzerland

Italian

French

German

Greek Language

Greek has been written and spoken for more than 3,000 years. It was the official language of the empire of Alexander the Great (4th century BC) and of the kingdom that followed, and later on of the Eastern Roman Empire up until the 15th century.

The Homeric poems, the *Iliad* and the *Odyssey,* which were originally part of an oral tradition, were written in Greek in about the 8th century BC, as were the great dramas in the 5th century BC. Works on medicine, philosophy, mathematics, history, and physical science were written much earlier in Greek than in any other European language. Many of the words used in these sciences come from Greek roots.

Ancient Greek is still studied in universities for its literary value and its contribution to history. The Greek spoken and used today is still based on the ancient language.

Map labels

NORWAY · SWEDEN · FINLAND · Gulf of Bothnia · gian · DENMARK · ERMANY · POLAND · CZECHOSLOVAKIA · AUSTRIA · ITZ · SLOVENIA · HUNGARY · CROATIA · ROMANIA · BOSNIA AND HERZEGOVINA · ITALY · YUGOSLAVIA · BULGARIA · ALBANIA · GREECE · Adriatic Sea · Black Sea · Aegean Sea · Sea · ean

0° · 10°E · 20°E · 30°E · 70°N · 60°N · 50°N · 40°N · 30°E · 20°E · °E

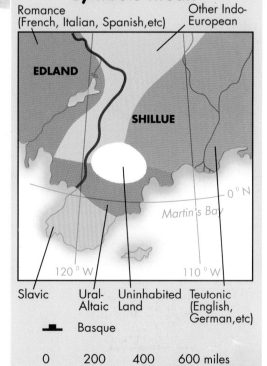

What the colors and symbols mean

Romance (French, Italian, Spanish, etc)

Other Indo-European

EDLAND

SHILLUE

Martin's Bay

120°W · 110°W · 0°N

Slavic · Ural-Altaic · Uninhabited Land · Teutonic (English, German, etc)

■ Basque

0 · 200 · 400 · 600 miles

Slang

Slang is the name given to words and phrases used only in very informal language or among a particular group of people. Colloquial speech is that used everyday or casually when there is no need to be formal.

Slang or colloquial language is used because it is more picturesque or because it expresses feelings more vividly than formal language. Groups that are together a lot, such as servicemen or theater companies, tend to develop their own slang.

London Cockneys are famous for rhyming slang, in which a word is replaced by another that rhymes with it, such as "apples and pears" for "stairs."

Abbreviated words are often found in slang, such as bike for bicycle. Words that were once slang may move slowly into accepted usage. Examples of these include "mob" and "bus."

The region's two main language groups are Teutonic and Romance. Teutonic languages like German, Dutch, and Danish dominate northern Europe, while Romance languages like French, Italian, and Spanish dominate southern Europe. English combines elements of both.

English Language

The English language gradually evolved over the years, and with the invention of the printing press and the spread of education, a concept of standard English helped to stabilize grammar and spelling. But English is a language that has continued to allow itself to be enriched by other cultures and languages. Today, as a language of science, literature, business, and commerce, it has few equals, and it probably gives more words to other languages than any other tongue.

French Language

One of the great languages of civilization, its ideas and words have been absorbed by many other languages all over the world. As early as the 12th century, French had a large and impressive literature. A feature of French is its nasal pronunciation of certain vowels — this is found in no other West European speech except Portuguese — and makes French sound very different.

Germanic Languages

Germanic is the basis of many European languages, including English, Scandinavian languages, German, and Dutch. German is one of the world's most important languages, with over 90 million people in Germany, Austria, and parts of Switzerland using it.

The British Sign Language

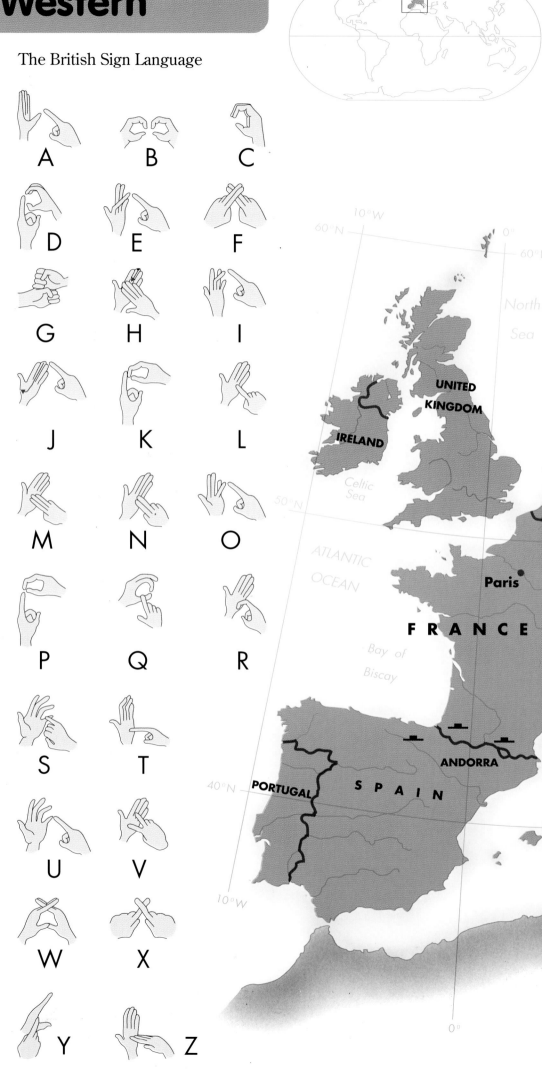

Breakdown of Languages in Belgium

German

French

Dutch

What the colors and symbols mean

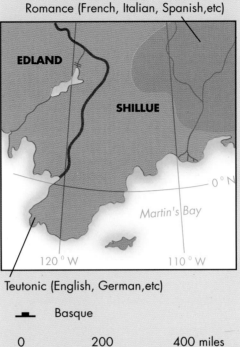

Romance (French, Italian, Spanish,etc)

EDLAND

SHILLUE

0°N

Martin's Bay

120°W   110°W

Teutonic (English, German,etc)

━▪━ Basque

0   200   400 miles

How many can read ?

A selection of countries in Western Europe.

Belgium

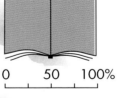

0   50   100%

Denmark

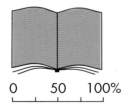

0   50   100%

France

0   50   100%

Germany

0   50   100%

Netherlands

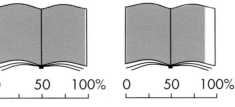

0   50   100%

Portugal

0   50   100%

Switzerland

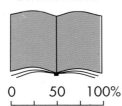

0   50   100%

United Kingdom

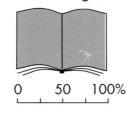

0   50   100%

Braille

Braille is a special alphabet for blind people, which they can use by feeling a pattern of raised lumps on paper. It was named for its inventor, Louis Braille (1809—52) who perfected this alphabet in 1834. It has not been widely used, however, until the last 20 years. Each letter consists of one or more raised dots, and there are six basic positions in which each dot can be placed. Therefore 63 different shapes are possible, 26 being used for the basic alphabet and the others for figures, punctuation, common words such as "the" or parts of words such as "ing." Blind people can write with a machine on which six dots in any combination can be written. This is called a Braille Writer. The paper is impressed from underneath, and as the bumps appear on the top of the paper the writing can be read as it is written.

An experienced reader can read aloud at conversational pace.

A-Z Alphabets

Braille

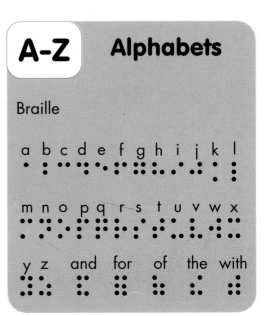

a b c d e f g h i j k l

m n o p q r s t u v w x

y z and for of the with

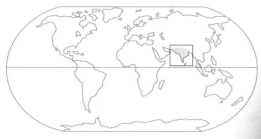

India, the main country of the area, has a huge number of languages. The major languages belong to two groups, Indo-European and Dravidian. Indo-European is spoken by three-quarters of the population of India.

Indian Language

The vast majority of people in northern India speak languages brought into India about 1400 BC by the Indo-Aryans, and so their language belongs to the same family as English.

About 400 BC the language was fixed by a great scholar named Panini, and under the name of Sanskrit it has continued throughout the ages to be the universal language of learning in India. Alongside this classical language many popular languages developed, the most important of which are Bengali, Oriya, Hindi, Kashmiri, Punjabi, Sindhi, Gujarati, and Marathi. Sinhalese, spoken in Sri Lanka, is also an Indo-Aryan language.

Urdu is an important language, spoken by the Muslim population and related to Arabic and Persian. Although Hindi and Urdu have become very different from one another, a compromise, understood by speakers of both has always been used in everyday speech: this is known as Hindustani. Since the formation of India and Pakistan, Urdu has been adopted as the official language of Pakistan and Hindi as that of India.

South India is dominated by Dravidian languages.

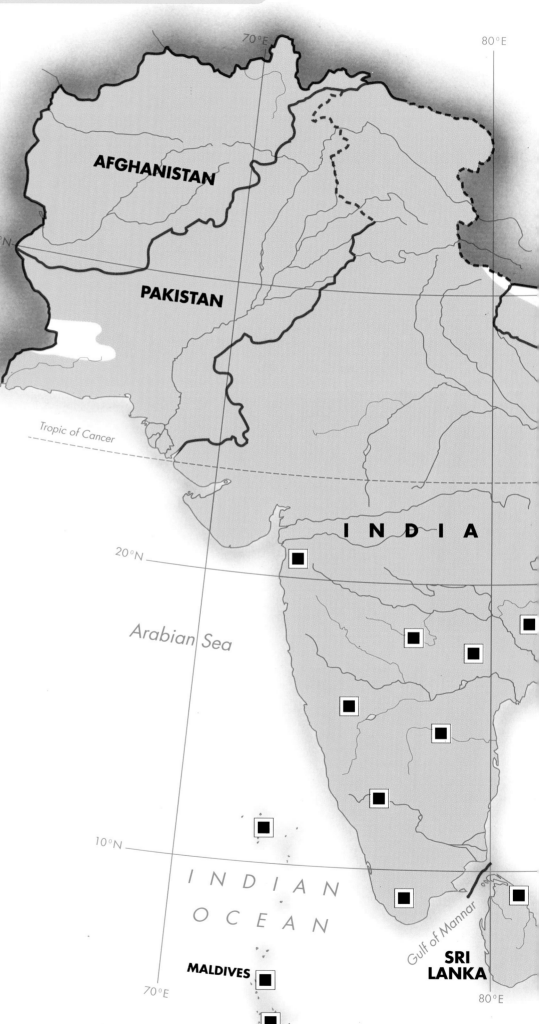

Amazing – But True

★ The total number of languages and dialects still spoken in the world is about 5,000, of which 845 come from India.

Breakdown of Languages in Pakistan

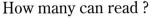

Urdu is the national language

Other
Urdu
Saraika
Sindhi
Pusto
Punjabi

How many can read ?

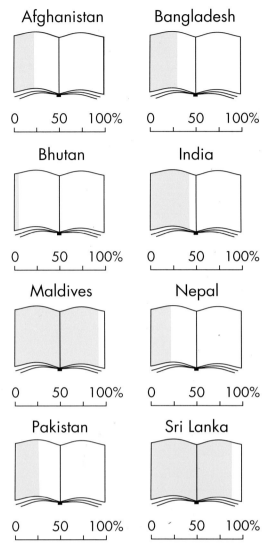

Afghanistan
0   50   100%

Bangladesh
0   50   100%

Bhutan
0   50   100%

India
0   50   100%

Maldives
0   50   100%

Nepal
0   50   100%

Pakistan
0   50   100%

Sri Lanka
0   50   100%

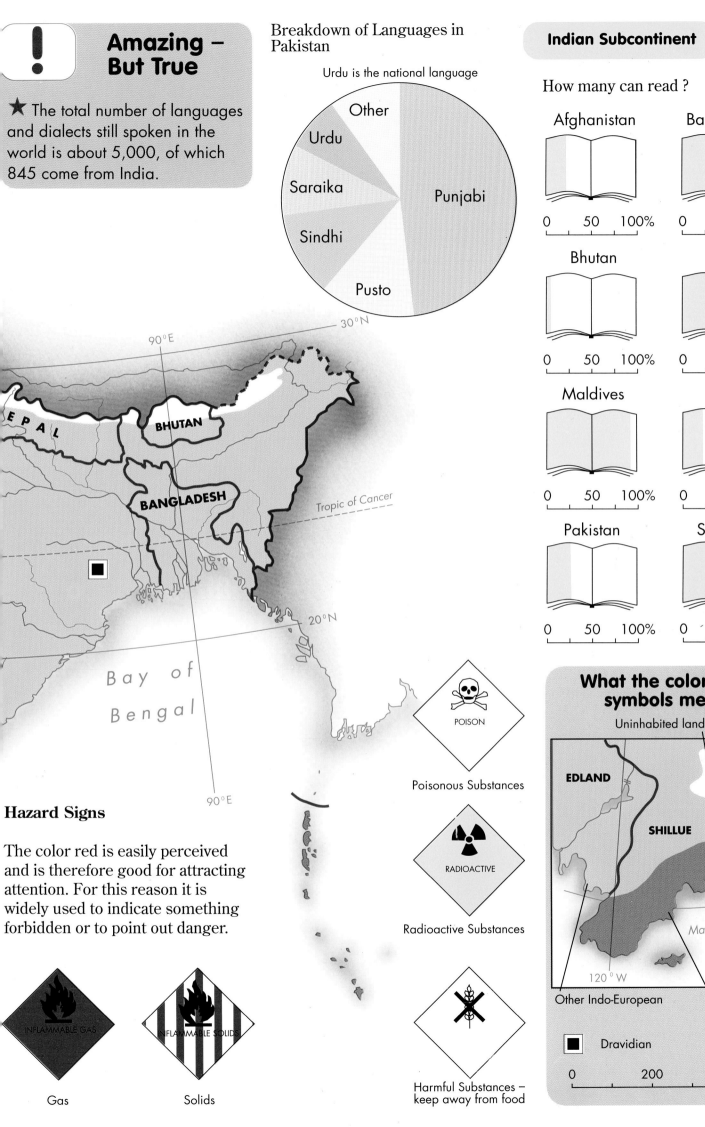

NEPAL

BHUTAN

BANGLADESH

Tropic of Cancer

Bay of Bengal

90°E

30°N

20°N

90°E

Hazard Signs

The color red is easily perceived and is therefore good for attracting attention. For this reason it is widely used to indicate something forbidden or to point out danger.

INFLAMMABLE GAS

Gas

INFLAMMABLE SOLIDS

Solids

POISON

Poisonous Substances

RADIOACTIVE

Radioactive Substances

Harmful Substances – keep away from food

What the colors and symbols mean

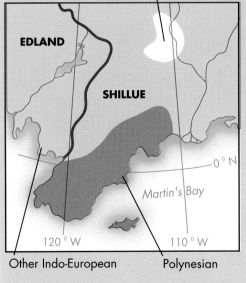

Uninhabited land

EDLAND

SHILLUE

Martin's Bay

0° N

120° W

110° W

Other Indo-European

Polynesian

■ Dravidian

0   200   400 miles

The Middle East is the origin of one of the most influential and widely spoken languages of the world — Arabic. Besides Arabic, other main languages used in the area include Hebrew, French, and English.

Semitic Languages

According to Hebrew tradition from the Book of Genesis, Semitic languages were those spoken by the descendants of the son of Noah, Shem. They were originally spoken in Mesopotamia, Syria, and Palestine and later spread to Egypt, Abyssinia and North Africa. Today the most important are Arabic, Hebrew, and Amharic.

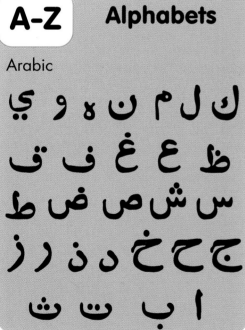

A-Z **Alphabets**

Arabic

ك ل م ن ه و ي

ظ غ ع ف ق

س ش ص ض ط

ج ح خ د ذ ر ز

ا ب ت ث

? **Did You Know**

★ Turkish and the languages of the Turkic peoples of the former Soviet Union are usually regarded as forming one family of languages. There are upward of 60 million speakers of Turkic languages.

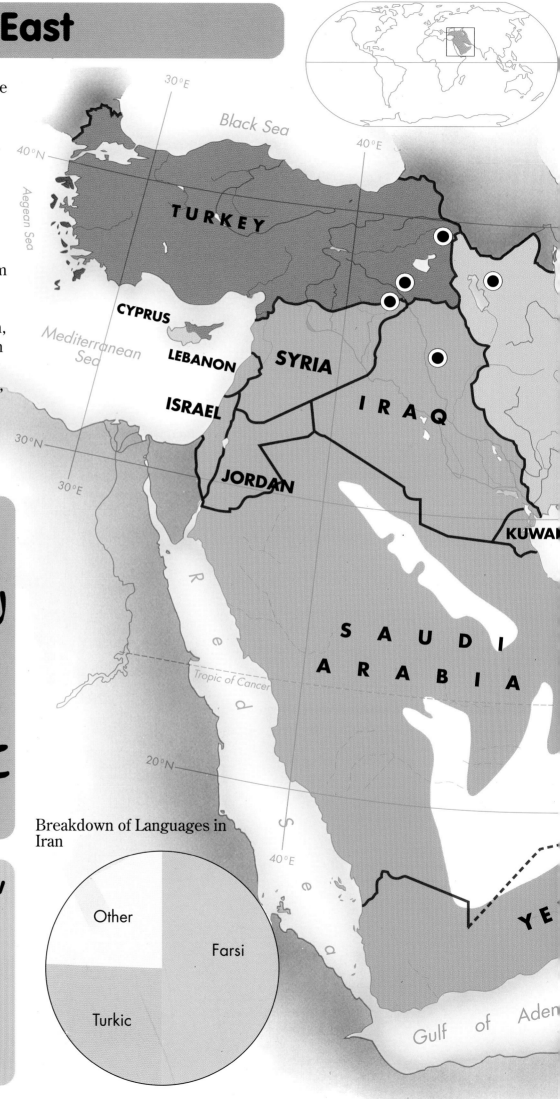

Breakdown of Languages in Iran

Other

Farsi

Turkic

How many can read ?

A selection of countries in the Middle East.

Bahrain

0   50   100%

Iran

0   50   100%

Iraq

0   50   100%

Israel

0   50   100%

Jordan

0   50   100%

Kuwait

0   50   100%

Lebanon

0   50   100%

Oman

0   50   100%

Saudi Arabia

0   50   100%

Syria

0   50   100%

Turkey

0   50   100%

Yemen

0   50   100%

Arabic Language

Arabic is the most widespread living representative of the Semitic languages, spread by the conquests of the Arabs in the 7th century and the later wanderings of the Bedouin tribes and the many Arab traders. It is spoken today by people in Iraq, Syria, Arabia, Egypt, and most of North Africa and northern Sudan. Although Arabic-speaking people are known as Arabs, they descend from many different races, and each country has its distinct dialect. It may be difficult for Arabs from one country to understand those from another; but what Arabic does have to unite it is one common written language based on classical Arabic. It is the language of the Koran, the sacred book of Islam, and of the Arabic literature of the Middle Ages, which was enormously rich in poetry and stories. The *Arabian Nights' Entertainments* is one of many famous Arabic books.

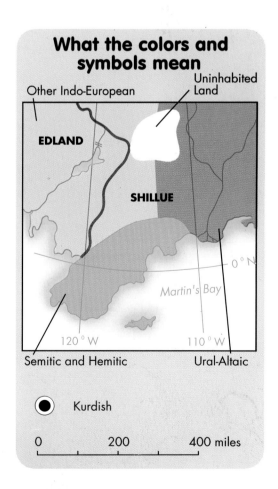

What the colors and symbols mean

Other Indo-European

Uninhabited Land

EDLAND

SHILLUE

Semitic and Hemitic

Ural-Altaic

120° W   110° W

0° N

Martin's Bay

⊙ Kurdish

0   200   400 miles

Oceania

Although Polynesian is probably the best known language in the region, Oceania includes numerous islands whose languages reflect the many different influences of the early settlers as well as indigenous populations.

How many can read ?

A selection of countries in Oceania.

Fiji

Tonga

| 0 | 50 | 100% |
| 0 | 50 | 100% |

140°E   150°E   160°E   170°E   180

10°N

Micronesia

Melanesia

Equator

0°

NAURU

SOLOMON ISLANDS

TUVALU

10°S   140°E

Solomon

Sea

Coral

Sea

VANUATU

FIJI

Breakdown of Languages in Fiji

20°S

Tropic of Capricorn

150°E

160°E

Hindi   Fijian

170°E   180

What the colors and symbols mean

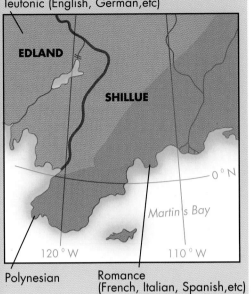

Teutonic (English, German, etc)

EDLAND

SHILLUE

Martin's Bay

Polynesian

Romance
(French, Italian, Spanish, etc)

| 0 | 200 | 400 | 600 miles |

Oceanic Languages

The Polynesians, Melanesians, and Micronesians speak languages that probably came to the Pacific Islands from the East Indies about 2,000 years ago.

Polynesian language uses only about ten consonants and six or seven vowels and has a simple and flexible grammar. Melanesian language, however, has elaborate grammatical rules and a vast number of sounds, many of which sound very unusual to our ears. A special feature of this language is the use of "chief's language,"

special words used only in communications with a chief. These languages vary considerably from island to island, but differences are gradually dying out with people mixing and communicating more. In many places Pidgin English is now spoken.

Pidgin-English

Pidgin languages are used for communication between groups of people who do not speak the same language. Pidgin languages have developed between English and Chinese, English and African, English and Melanesian, as well as between other languages such as Russian and Norwegian (Russonorsk) and French and West African languages. When such a language drives out the mother tongue, as in Haiti, the language is called "Creole."
Pidgin English strikes English speakers as being very amusing, because it is so like English, yet not English.

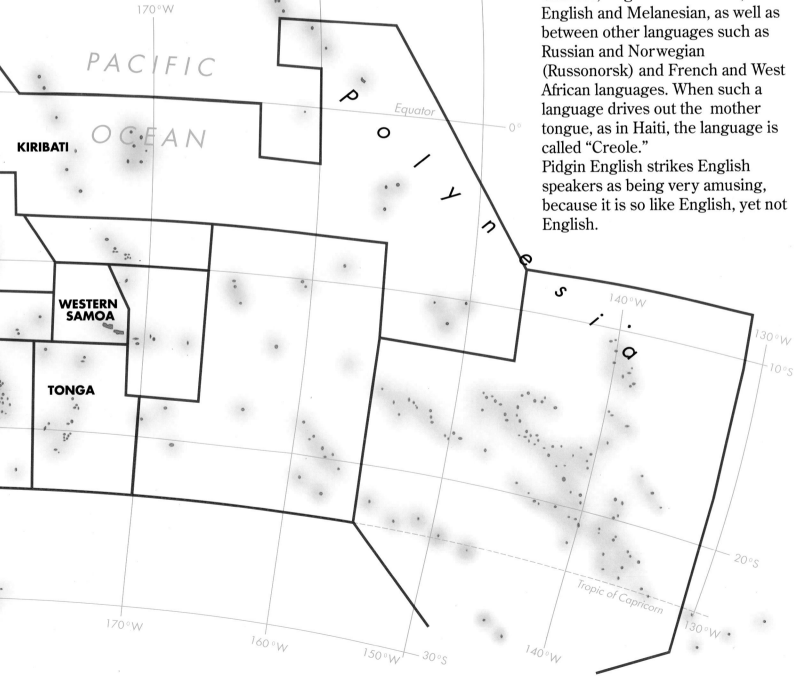

PACIFIC

OCEAN

KIRIBATI

WESTERN SAMOA

TONGA

Polynesia

Equator

Tropic of Capricorn

Two distinct groups dominate the U.S. First, the many American Indian languages, which are in danger of dying out, and second, the languages of the mostly European colonists from the 17th century onward.

United Nations

The United Nations was founded on October 24, 1945, after the end of World War II. The nations of the world had decided that they must work together to prevent a world war ever happening again. The UN charter was drawn up in San Francisco on June 26, 1945, and had been signed by the 51 founder members, including the United States. In the charter, the countries of the United Nations promised to live in peace, be united in their strength so as to maintain peace and security in the world, and ensure that armed force should only be used if they all agreed to it. The United Nations have increased their numbers from 51 to about 180 countries or member states.

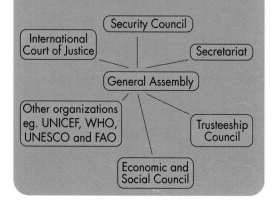

United Nations

The United Nations is divided into six main sections. The political sections are based at the United Nations headquarters in New York. Most other branches and agencies are based in Europe.

- International Court of Justice
- Security Council
- Secretariat
- General Assembly
- Other organizations eg. UNICEF, WHO, UNESCO and FAO
- Trusteeship Council
- Economic and Social Council

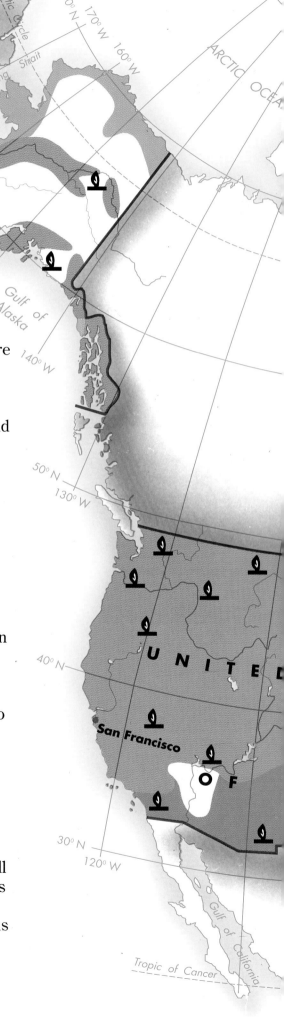

Within the United Nations there are many organizations that help the world with different problems.

The United Nations Childrens Fund (UNICEF) helps children in the poor countries of the world.

The World Health Organization (WHO) concentrates on providing high standards of health for all people through its 850 research centers.

The United Nations Educational Scientific and Cultural Organization (UNESCO) aims to help countries make better use of their resources and improve education so that illiteracy is reduced. It also helps to preserve monuments to help countries keep their heritage.

The Food and Agricultural Organization (FAO) aims to improve nutrition, standards of living, and distribution of all food. The FAO is trying to ensure that all the world has food and no one goes hungry.
There are many more organizations within the United Nations that spend their time helping improve the world for tomorrow's children.

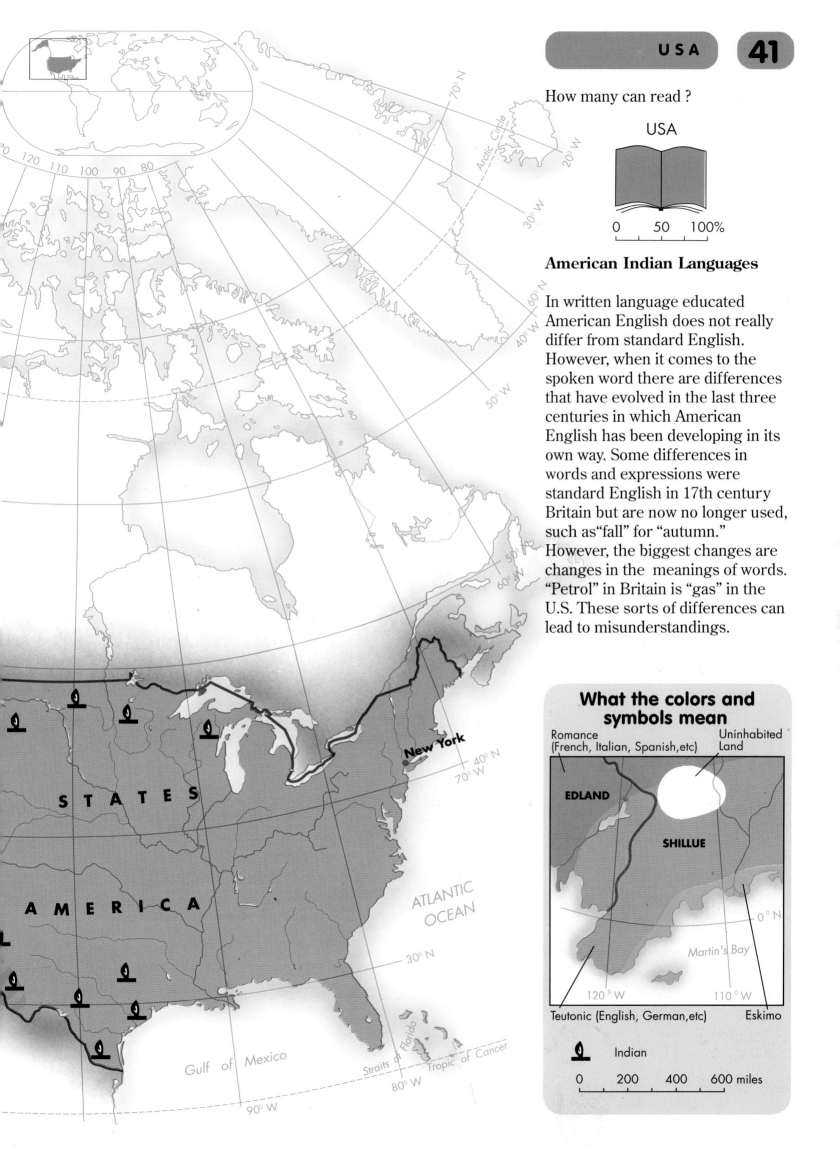

How many can read ?

USA

0   50   100%

American Indian Languages

In written language educated American English does not really differ from standard English. However, when it comes to the spoken word there are differences that have evolved in the last three centuries in which American English has been developing in its own way. Some differences in words and expressions were standard English in 17th century Britain but are now no longer used, such as "fall" for "autumn." However, the biggest changes are changes in the meanings of words. "Petrol" in Britain is "gas" in the U.S. These sorts of differences can lead to misunderstandings.

New York

STATES

AMERICA

ATLANTIC OCEAN

Gulf of Mexico

What the colors and symbols mean

Romance (French, Italian, Spanish, etc)

Uninhabited Land

EDLAND

SHILLUE

Martin's Bay

Teutonic (English, German, etc)

Eskimo

Indian

0   200   400   600 miles

Article
A short word, occurring in many languages, that lacks any specific meaning but acts as a determiner. *The* and *a* are articles.

Caucasian
A person belonging to a racial group that is characterized by a light-colored complexion. This group includes the peoples of Europe and North Africa.

Characters
Symbols used in a writing system, including letters of an alphabet or a Chinese pictographs.

Colloquial
Informal or spoken use of a language, as contrasted with more formal written use.

Consonants
Letters of the alphabet other than the vowels.

Cyrillic alphabet
The alphabet now used mainly for Russian and Bulgarian, said to have been devised by Saint Cyril.

Dialect
A form of language spoken in a particular geographical area or by members of a specific social class. It is distinguished by its grammar, vocabulary, and pronunciation and may be considered a subgroup of the main language.

Gender
Grammatical categories of masculine, feminine, and neuter into which the nouns of a language may be categorized.

Inflection
Changes in the modulation of the voice when pronouncing the same word, thus giving it different meanings.

Mother tongue
The first language learned by a child.

Nasal
A tone pronounced with the soft palate of the mouth lowered, allowing air to escape via the nose.

Phonetic
A speech sound.

Pictograph
A symbol or picture standing for a word or a group of words, such as in written Chinese.

Pidgin
A language made up of elements of two languages or more. Many of these languages developed between speakers of different tongues to facilitate trading.

Roman alphabet
The alphabet that was developed by the ancient Romans for writing Latin. It originated with the Phoenicians and now serves for writing most of the languages of Western Europe.

Script
The letters, characters, and figures used in handwriting.

Semaphore
A system of signaling by holding a flag in each hand and moving the arms to designated positions for each letter of the alphabet.

Semitic
A branch of the Afro–Asian family of languages that includes Arabic, Hebrew, and such ancient languages as Phoenician.

Syllables
Units of sound that combine to form a word. For example, the word *baby* has two syllables.

Tenses
Different forms of a verb, such as past, present, and future, which express differences in time.

Teutonic
Relating to the German language.

Tone
The pitch or level at which a syllable may be pronounced.

Vocabulary
All the words contained in a language.

Vowels
Sounds in speech characterized by the absence of any obstruction in the vocal passages, allowing a free passage of air.

Bolinger, Dwight. *Aspects of Language.*
New York: Harcourt Brace Jovanovich, 1968.

Burgess, Anthony. *Language Made Plain: An Introduction to the Study of Language and Languages.*
New York: Crowell, 1964.

Chaika, Elaine. *Language: The Social Mirror.*
Rowley, M.A.: Newbury House, 1988.

Davidson, Jessica. *Is That Mother in the Bottle? Where Language Came From and Where It Is Going.*
New York: Watts, 1972.

Edwards, E. W. *Exploring Careers Using Foreign Languages.*
Rev. ed. New York: Rosen, 1986.

Firth, J. R. *The Tongues of Men and Speech.*
London: Oxford University Press, 1964.

Huebener, Theodore. *Opportunities in Foreign Language Careers.*
Skokie, I.L.: National Textbook Company, 1981.

Katzner, Kenneth. *The Languages of the World.*
New York: Funk & Wagnalls, 1975.

Ogg, Oscar. *The 26 Letters.*
Rev. ed. New York: Crowell, 1971.

Pei, Mario. *The Story of Language.*
New York: Meridian, 1965.

Potter, Simeon. *Language in the Modern World.*
Rev. ed. London: Andre Deutsch, 1975.

This index is designed to help you to find places shown on the maps. The index is in alphabetical order and lists all towns, countries, and physical features. After each entry extra information is given to describe the entry and to tell you which country or continent it is in.

The next column contains the latitude and longitude figures. These are used to help locate places on maps. They are measured in degrees. The blue lines drawn across the map are lines of latitude. The equator is at latitude 0°. All lines above the equator are referred to as °N (north of the equator). All lines below the equator are referred to as °S (south of the equator).

The blue lines drawn from the top to the bottom of the map are lines of longitude. The 0° line passes through Greenwich, London, and is known as the Greenwich Meridian. All lines of longitude join the North Pole to the South Pole. All lines to the right of the Greenwich Meridian are referred to as °E (east of Greenwich), and all lines to the left of the Greenwich Meridian are referred to as °W (west of Greenwich).

The final column indicates the number of the page where you will find the place for which you are searching.

If you want to find out where the Gulf of Thailand is, look it up in the alphabetical index. The entry will read:

Name, Description	Location	Page
	Lat. Long.	
Thailand, Gulf of, Asia	11°N 101°E	22

Turn to page 22 in your atlas. The Gulf of Thailand is located where latitude 11°N meets longitude 101°E. Place a pencil along latitude 11°N. Now take another pencil and place it along 101°E. Where the two pencils meet is the location of the Gulf of Thailand. Practice finding places in the index and on the maps.

Scott E. Morris is an associate professor of geography at the University of Idaho, where his current areas of teaching and research interest include mountain geomorphology, field methods, and human impact on the landscape process. Dr. Morris received his Ph.D. from the University of Colorado, Boulder, and has published prolifically on the formation and climatic history of mountain landscapes, the effects of wildfire and mineral resource extraction on soil erosion processes, and the influence of water diversion and channel modification on sediment transport.